EVERYONE'S GUIDE TO SOUTH AFRICAN BIRDS

Photographs by Peter Johnson

Text by John Sinclair and John Mendelsohn

cna

PHOTOGRAPHER'S ACKNOWLEDGEMENTS
At the outset I must thank Walther Votteler whose conceptual skills and
superb design have given a special quality to this as well as my previous
books.

Without the affection and loyalty of Claire, my wife, and Susan, my 12-
year-old daughter, projects such as this would be impossible; whilst the
help, friendship, kindness and hospitality that I have received from Pam
Barlow, Alex and Sheila Camerer, John Cooper, the Badenhorst Durrants,
Richard and Margot Gawith, Johan Groenewald, Alison Inglis, Walter
Mangold, Mordaunt and Kate Milner, Roy Siegfried and Jack Winterbottom
made the task the greatest fun and success. I am indebted to Norman
Elwell, Walter Stanford, Hugh Chittenden and Neville Brickell for the loan
of the pictures of the pale-winged starling, Natal robin, puff-back shrike
and black-cheeked waxbill, respectively, the four species which I did not
have on file for this book.

Finally, the most professional 'twitcher' in the business, John Sinclair,
go my thanks for putting together the essentials of what the sport of
'twitching' is all about.

PHOTOGRAPHER'S DEDICATION
To my Godmother – Peggy Francis.

AUTHORS' ACKNOWLEDGEMENTS
Dr P.A. Clancey is thanked for his donation of the immature ringed
plover painting on page 11. For the fine job of editing our manuscript,
Peter Borchert is due our sincere thanks.

AUTHORS' DEDICATION
To our wives, Jacqueline and Celia.

CENTRAL NEWS AGENCY (PTY) LTD
CNA BUILDING, LAUB STREET,
NEW CENTRE, JOHANNESBURG 2001

REG. NO.: 01/02033/06

FIRST EDITION 1981
SECOND IMPRESSION 1984
THIRD IMPRESSION 1985
FOURTH IMPRESSION 1986
FIFTH IMPRESSION 1987
SIXTH IMPRESSION 1988
SEVENTH IMPRESSION 1989

COPYRIGHT © PHOTOGRAPHS: PETER JOHNSON
COPYRIGHT © TEXT: JOHN SINCLAIR AND JOHN MENDELSOHN

DESIGN BY W. VOTTELER, CAPE TOWN
LITHOGRAPHIC REPRODUCTION BY UNIFOTO (PTY) LTD, CAPE TOWN
PHOTOSET BY PHOTOPRINTS (PTY) LTD, CAPE TOWN
PRINTED AND BOUND BY TIEN WAH PRESS PTE LTD, SINGAPORE

ISBN 0 620 05218 X

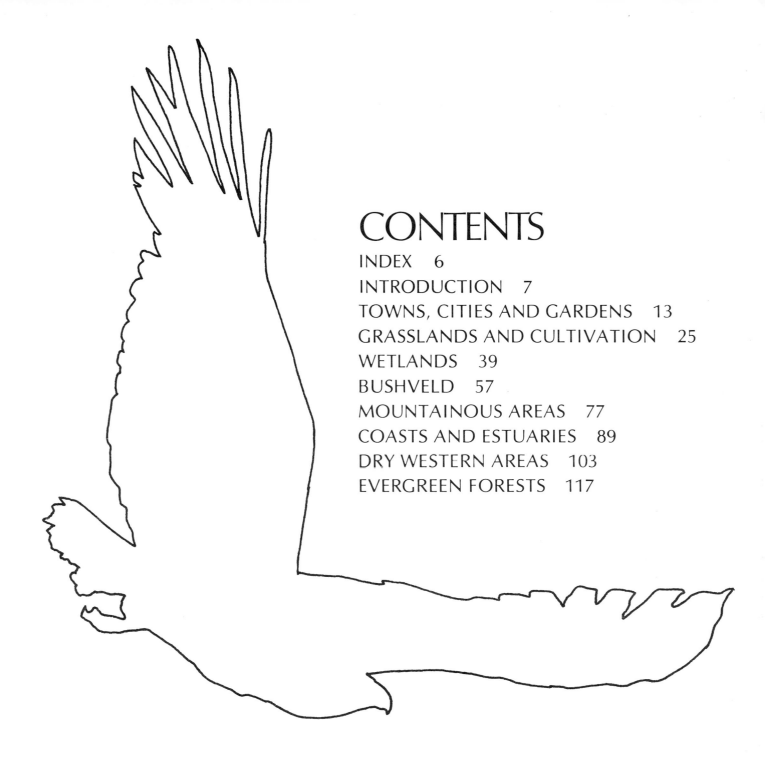

CONTENTS

FURTHER READING
The following books are recommended to readers requiring further information on South African birds.

McLachlan, G.R. & Liversidge, R. 1978. *Roberts Birds of South Africa*, Cape Town: John Voelcker Bird Book Fund.
Newman, K.B. 1980. *Birds of Southern Africa. 1. Kruger National Park*, Johannesburg : MacMillan.
Newman, K.B. (ed.). 1979. *Birdlife in Southern Africa*, MacMillan.
Clancey, P.A. (ed.). 1980. *S.A.O.S. Checklist of Southern African Birds*, Johannesburg : Southern African Ornithological Society.
Cyrus, D. & N. Robson. 1980. *Bird Atlas of Natal*, Pietermaritzburg : University of Natal Press.
Winterbottom, J.M. 1971. *Priest's Eggs of Southern African Birds*, Johannesburg : Winchester Press.

INDEX

6

INTRODUCTION

More than 800 species of birds – a tenth of all those known to man – are found in South Africa. Few regions in the world can boast such an avian paradise. The reasons for this wealth are simply explained in the diversity of the natural environment. Consider the nutrient-rich Benguela Current which sweeps by to the west of the country; the verdant coastal forests of Tsitsikama and Zululand; and the eruption of life in the arid west after a sudden and infrequent downpour. Consider, too, the ragged ranges that all but encircle the endless rolling grassland and bushveld of the central massif. South Africa, in fact, provides a scaled-down version of the whole continent since practically all the major habitats of Africa are represented in this relatively small region south of the Limpopo River.

Biologists and naturalists became truly aware of this great wealth towards the end of the Eighteenth Century when, in keeping with the burgeoning desire to find 'curiosities' so in vogue at the time, dilettante collectors, amateurs in the finest of traditions, first visited the country. The efforts of these intrepid 'explorers' are remembered in many of the names given to our birds. Their spirit of amateurism, too, persists for, spurred on by the vast number of books on the subject and the availability of relatively inexpensive binoculars and photographic equipment, bird watching, or the commonly used term 'birding', has developed into a popular pastime.

For the enthusiastic birder in South Africa, the vast variety of both resident and migrant birds always holds some as-yet-unseen species to be identified and watched. To see even 75 percent of the birds present in South Africa may take a keen observer a lifetime. But birding in a city suburb or even during a casual day-trip into the countryside can produce close to a hundred different species.

Some people would also say that finding and identifying a new bird is a way of satisfying a 'hunting' urge inherent in us all. Man's wish to collect things is also expressed in birding by his compiling of lists of birds seen in different localities and countries. Some find it fascinating to collect feathers, if only for the challenge of identifying which birds they come from; or take it one step further, to collect feathers from as many different species as possible. Photography can be another form of collecting. But parallel to, and developing from, man's desire to collect, is his desire to understand, and for many birders identification is not the end, but the first tentative step towards a deeper and infinitely more meaningful knowledge of the behaviour of birds. In any form, however, birding is a healthy outdoor activity to be enjoyed equally by young and old.

As a casual beginner or enthusiastic amateur this book will help you to identify 200 of the more common birds found in South Africa. It will also set a base for you to tackle the remaining species while introducing some of the fascinating details of the lives of our birds. Such words as

'common' and 'rare' are, however, relative and more often than not, descriptive of a bird's habits rather than its abundance. Thus huge vultures soaring about the bushveld may appear more common than secretive warblers, while in fact, the warblers hidden in the undergrowth far outnumber the thermal-riding scavengers.

Most bird books dealing with southern Africa consider all species found south of the Zambezi and Cunene rivers. In limiting the scope of this book to South Africa, we have introduced those species which birdwatchers, with some effort and a few, well-planned vacations, should be able to spot with relative ease.

Most birds favour certain environments above others and, in grouping the species illustrated and discussed in this book, we have borne this general observation in mind. In some cases these preferences are undoubtedly concerned with the historical origins of the birds, and thus, for example, we would never conceive of an albatross living in the forest. For others though, a range of habitats is available and these birds tend to choose the areas which offer the best chances of survival and therefore of successful breeding. These, however, are theoretical considerations only, and it is seldom clear on what basis such choices are made. Some important environmental factors may include the type of food, the height and density of the vegetation, and the temperatures experienced in the area.

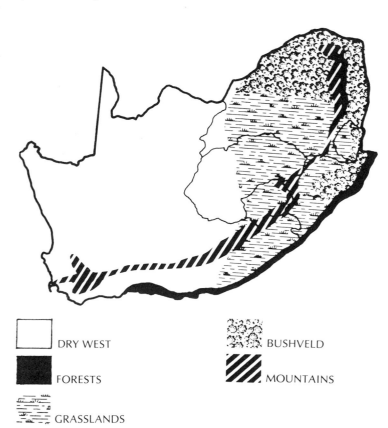

☐ DRY WEST	BUSHVELD
■ FORESTS	MOUNTAINS
GRASSLANDS	

The eight habitat categories selected for this book are probably the broadest and most distinct groupings for South Africa. The distribution of our grasslands, bushveld, dry west country and some of the mountainous and forest areas are shown on the accompanying map. There are many other smaller forests and mountainous areas which, together with the wetlands, are more widely distributed throughout the country. Similarly, agricultural areas and town gardens transcend such broad categories. In the introduction to each chapter we give the localities where the most characteristic birds of that particular habitat are likely to be seen.

It is possible to divide habitats into finer groupings, for example into lowland and high-altitude forest. But many of our birds do not obey such fine, human-devised limitations and, in addition, some birds move between habitats on a seasonal, or even a daily basis. Birds living at high altitudes often move out of mountainous areas in winter to lower-lying country where temperatures are less harsh and food more abundant. Many forest birds such as the hadeda ibis make regular foraging excursions to other habitats near by, returning only to the forest to tend their nests and to roost.

The face of South Africa has been greatly altered, particularly during this century. The intrusion of man, his animals and machines have progressively changed or cut back vast tracts of natural environment to little more than residual 'islands'. There has been a rapid eastward march of Karoo-type veld, as grasslands in the Orange Free State and eastern Cape have been destroyed by overgrazing and soil erosion. Forested areas have been markedly reduced in size to make way for pastures and crops. In Natal, huge seas of undulating sugar-cane plantations now replace forests and primeval marshes; while immense plantations of pines, gums and poplars now stand where indigenous grasslands and forests once sprawled for thousands of years. These exotic trees seldom provide agreeable habitats for most South African birds, there being few insects and other suitable food resources in such uniform environments. And the nutrient-sapping roots of these rapidly-growing trees prevent the nourishment of undergrowth which would also harbour many insects and other small animals.

While such situations provide cause for concern and make it vitally important that we prevent the total destruction of natural habitats, birds like man and many other animals can, within reason, adapt. In recent times, the only bird lost to extinction in South Africa has been the yellow-billed oxpecker. Often, where natural habitats have been replaced with others, some birds have been able to exploit the new environments. Agricultural areas and urban settings alike, have provided new homes for a variety of creatures.

This is particularly true of insects that capitalize on garden plants and crops to such a degree that some are now considered pests. Only a handful of bird species ever present such 'problems' and most of these arise from man's misunderstanding and ignorance – also because, unwittingly, he has provided ideal and abundant food which certain species will 'expand' to exploit. For example, red-billed queleas often reach pest proportions because they now take advantage of the vast grain-producing croplands that cover immense tracts in South Africa. These birds undoubtedly pose a real threat to the farmer with a bank account to balance. Damage to some grain crops may be severe and controls are often necessary. With little or no justification, however, our birds of prey are frequently treated as vermin and pronounced guilty of thieving chickens and other small domestic stock without any evidence whatsoever.

The majority of birds can, fortunately, live peacefully alongside man without any conflict. In towns, such birds add colour to the concrete maze of streets and buildings and we later suggest how a garden can be planned to attract a variety of birds. Before this, however, one further facet of the environment and its attendant bird-life should be considered.

Irrespective of how well some birds may adapt to the new environments thrust upon them, undisturbed habitats that have existed unaltered for thousands of years are generally richest in the numbers of different species. In such environments the variety of separate micro-habitats is great, and different birds have the opportunity of occupying many distinct niches without competing directly with one another. This situation is perhaps most clearly illustrated in natural forests where different birds are divided according to what they eat and where they forage and nest. Some glean insects and fruit from the canopy foliage, others hop around the leaf litter on the forest floor, while yet others creep along trunks and large branches, probing for insects in the bark.

When watching birds it is always useful to try to identify the roles of different species. It is then that the birder begins a real awareness of the intricate mesh that links the lives of all plants and animals. This is the substance of the natural environment that man should strive to preserve.

Each structural aspect of a bird's body has a specific and critical role to play in the functioning of the animal, be it in flying, feeding, hunting, mating or even maintaining its body temperature. In an analogous way, birds also have an array of behavioural patterns that assist in breeding, feeding and many other facets of their lives. Much of this behaviour is seen to revolve around communication, and it is true that birds spend a lot of time and energy transferring information between members of the same and different species. The methods of doing so can be highly distinctive, with many species having evolved a number of stereotyped calls and plumage patterns that separate them from all others. Sound and visual signals predominate in the language of birds, for unlike many mammals, they probably do not use chemical excretions or smells for communication. Birds, too, have good eyesight and can distinguish colours. Often-bright plumages, therefore, frequently serve as 'semaphore' signals of aggression, submission or availability for breeding. Many plumages are divided into two components, one cryptic and the other highly conspicuous. Examples of cryptic feathering are the drab grey plumage of most doves and the plain-coloured backs of longclaws and bush shrikes. Yet, the same birds can display very bright parts of their plumages; for instance, the black and white tail-feathers of doves, and the striking yellow, oranges and reds on the breasts of longclaws and bush shrikes. Cryptic feathering generally protects birds against detection by predators, while the bright flashes are exposed at will to communicate with others of their own kind. A scrub robin can move undetected through the undergrowth, and then suddenly on encountering a mate or intruder, flash its white tail-feathers by opening and closing its tail.

During the breeding season, many of the males of these nondescript birds forsake the safety of their cryptic colours and don sometimes splendid dress. This phenomenon is often combined with conspicuous display flights and distinctive calls. It serves to advertise the bird's presence to prospective mates and as a signal to would-be competitors that they are entering an already-established domain. At such times these birds may be more vulnerable to predation, but for a time at least, the need to procreate outweighs the need for discretion. It is interesting that it is usually only the male that undergoes such a transformation – the female remains drab and inconspicuous, ideally suited, in fact, for her role of remaining undetected while incubating her clutch of eggs.

Birds that live in forests, marshes and grasslands usually have rather loud calls. In these environments, but for the brief breeding splendour of some species, visual signals are of limited use since birds are often invisible at distances of more than one or two metres. Sound is the most obvious and characteristic means by which these birds advertise their presence to one another. Some familiar examples are the 'piet-my-vrou' of the red-chested cuckoo, the 'dee...dee... diederik' of the diederik cuckoo, and the endless cooing of many doves. The information transferred in such calls can be substantial and may signify the species identity, the sex and the position of the individual caller.

Recently, it has been suggested that some calls may even serve to deceive other birds. Thus, robins that mimic the calls, of many other bird species, may falsely create an impression that the area is already crowded. On hearing this great range of calls, a newcomer may then be dissuaded from settling in the apparently heavily-populated area. A strategy of this nature would undoubtedly benefit the mimic by ensuring that few competitors settle in the immediate vicinity, but this and other ideas await substantiation. There may also be some merit in suggesting that the seemingly monotonous calls of some birds may not simply repeat the same information.

While the vocabulary of birds and the range of plumages they display are usually standard for each species, feeding and breeding behaviour are often highly variable. It is becoming more and more evident that individuals make decisions concerning the best ways to feed, the safest places to nest and whether or not to defend territories. It is not yet clear how such decisions are made, but there is abundant evidence that birds can assess the costs and benefits of various courses of action.

Bird parties typify the feeding strategy of many forest and bush birds in South Africa. These loose associations include as many as fifteen different species; some birds drop out, while others join the communal food hunt as it moves through the woodland canopy. Bird parties probably aid the members in finding widely-dispersed food sources as well as providing vigilance against predators. The principle is that the large number of eyes working in co-operation is able to detect food and predators more easily and rapidly than could a single bird.

Environmental factors such as food supply, temperature, rainfall and day length are forever changing. These may occur seasonally, weekly, daily or even hourly. As a result, certain periods are favourable for some birds while others are hazardous. For example, food may be only temporarily abundant, very high or low temperatures impose a stress on birds attempting to regulate their body temperatures; and short days limit the time available for foraging or hunting. These fluctuations mean that birds must time their activities so that the most advantageous conditions are exploited for their most demanding activities.

Breeding is one such stressful activity because birds require extra food and energy to produce eggs and to feed their young. Timing is vital, as inexperienced young birds need to be launched into the world when they can find food most easily. For these reasons, most South African birds start breeding in spring and fledge their young later in summer. The details of timing vary slightly between species to suit individual breeding cycles, the number of broods raised in a single season and to synchronize with the precise time when their preferred foods are most abundant. The start of breeding may also be delayed, especially if summer rains arrive late.

There are some interesting exceptions to the general trend of summer breeding. Birds living in desert and semi-desert areas are strongly dependent on rainfall since food only becomes abundant after a good soaking. In these areas rain is characteristically unpredictable and desert birds have therefore adapted their reproductive biology so that they start breeding immediately after rain, irrespective of the time of year. A good fall of rain on the parched desert ground will result in stimulated plant growth, and several weeks later there will be abundant seed for the seed-eaters and an associated flush of insects for the insectivores. A good insect supply is also important for most seed-eaters whose nestlings are fed on a diet of insects.

There are several ways in which animals avoid harsh conditions, particularly the cold, food-scarce months of winter. Many mammals hibernate and a few migrate short distances to better areas. It is not surprising, with their impressive flight abilities, that a great number of birds move between different regions, either on a regular or sporadic basis. We have already mentioned movements from high altitude areas to low-lying country. These movements are most prevalent in the east where birds move away from the Drakensberg range to winter on the temperate coastal belt of Natal and Moçambique. But these migrations are insignificant when compared with the epic pole-to-pole journeys undertaken by some. The Arctic tern, for instance, may cover 10 000 to 20 000 kilometres each year in its massive trek to and from the Arctic circle.

Each summer, South African avifauna receives a massive injection as millions of migrants flood the country from Europe, Asia, from the sub-Antarctic region and from further north in Africa. There are basically two groups of migrants to South Africa: those that breed here and those that do not. The former group, mainly the intra-African migrants, includes several swallows, cuckoos and swifts, while the majority of birds from further afield that visit us are non-breeders. Some familiar migrants from Europe and Asia include the European swallow, white stork and steppe buzzard. Migrants from the sub-Antarctic comprise mainly albatrosses, petrels and skuas.

The vast majority of land birds that visit South Africa are insectivorous, an indication of the great proliferation of this natural food source during our summer months.

Local migration and nomadism are less obvious, but nevertheless very prevalent forms of bird movement in South Africa. A good deal of the region is dry and, with unpredictable rainfall conditions, many birds move around to exploit temporary flushes of food. Predominant groups in this category are the larks and several raptors and sunbirds. If successive visits are made to the northern Cape, the birder will probably notice that on one visit an area is almost devoid of life, yet, returning several weeks later, the whole area may be humming with displaying birds starting to breed.

Birds are generally known by their vernacular names, and understandably so. For these popular names are, after all, the ones we grew up with and the ones most comprehensible to us. Unfortunately, these names can also be the source of great confusion as, more often than not, a bird is known by different names throughout its range. For example, a bird known in South Africa as a laughing dove may be known as a palm dove in Europe, while the name little brown dove may be in common usage in India.

Even within comparatively short distances, names can differ. In a multi-lingual country like South Africa, the problem is exacerbated as each language may have its own set of common names. The fiscal shrike provides a good example. Known in English as the fiscal, Jackie Hangman or butcher-bird, in Afrikaans it is labelled *Jan Fiskaal* or *Laksman*. To the Zulu, this same shrike is known as *i-Lunga,* to the Xhosa *inxanxadi;* and to the Sotho as *tsemeli.*

To avoid such confusion, scientists have developed rules for the naming of all organisms throughout the plant and animal kingdoms. Known as the 'International Code of Zoological Nomenclature', this system had its beginning in the work of the Swedish naturalist Carl von Linné who, in 1758, gave the first standard, or Latin, names to the plants and animals sent to him by collectors from all over the world – he even Latinized his own name to Linnaeus.

Returning to the example of the fiscal shrike, its Latin, or more properly, its scientific name, consists of two parts. The first, or generic name *Lanius* indicates that this bird is linked through evolution to other, similar shrikes which bear the same name. The second, or specific, name *collaris* denotes the bird's distinctness and separates it from all others in the genus. Thus *Lanius collaris* is unique to the fiscal shrike throughout the world. It is always written in italics.

Binominal nomenclature, as this double-naming system is known, is only part of a much broader system used to classify all living organisms. The plant and animal kingdoms are the broadest of these and both are broken down into smaller and smaller groups, each having certain common characteristics.

During the Eighteenth Century, many naturalists visiting South Africa had their introduction to the land, its flora and fauna, via Cape Town and Durban and, understandably, the first bird specimens were collected within the bounds of these emergent ports. Such specimens were usually despatched to Europe for description and naming and therefore many of our birds bear the specific names *capensis* or *natalensis,* labels not necessarily appropriate to their distribution.

Among these early collectors were men like Le Vaillant and Wahlberg who are remembered in the names of birds such as Levaillant's cisticola and Wahlberg's eagle. The scientists to whom they sent their 'finds', men like Gmelin, Temminck and even Linnaeus himself, are also reflected in the names of our birds.

Today, very few, if any, birds remain unnamed in Africa and science has progressed from mere description to more meaningful research into the understanding of birds and the wonderful ways in which they organize their lives.

Just as the natural environment provides different birds with food, shelter and nesting sites, so the enthusiastic bird-watcher can encourage many bird species to make their homes in, or at least visit, his or her garden. The equation is simple – the more varied the contents of the garden the greater will be the number of bird species to visit it.

Standard items are bird feeders and birdbaths which, especially during winter, will attract birds from far and wide. A bird table is easily constructed and even a dustbin lid turned upside down will serve as a handy birdbath. Both table and bath should, however, be placed in the shade to prevent the contents from drying out too rapidly. Food scraps placed on the bird table should be varied to attract as many different species as possible. For example, chopped fruit will attract mousebirds, bulbuls, barbets and even loeries, while different seeds will draw canaries, buntings, waxbills and the ubiquitous sparrows. Concentrated sugar-water placed in a water dispenser, such as that used for a pet budgie and positioned in a tree, will soon have colourful sunbirds in attendance. Sunbirds are generally attracted by bright flowers, and by painting the water dispenser vivid yellow, orange or red, it may prove more of a drawcard to these nectar feeders.

A few really keen birdwatchers plant indigenous trees and shrubs in their gardens. Apart from being most attractive and certainly the equal of many exotic plants, they help to simulate a natural environment for birds. Many of these plants produce berries which are included in the natural diet of most fruit-eating birds. Indigenous shrubs and trees also attract a wealth of insect life, thus providing a varied menu for many small predatory birds. Aloes and proteas in particular will enable sunbirds to enjoy real nectar instead of an artificial substitute in a dispenser.

The success of indigenous plants in your garden depends on the prevailing climate. The following is a list of trees and shrubs that can be grown readily in various regions. It does not pretend to be complete and your local nursery will be able to suggest many others.

Frost-free coastal Natal, eastern Cape and eastern Transvaal.
Tree fuschia, *Halleria lucida* – evergreen tree
Pigeon wood, *Trema orientalis* – evergreen tree
White stinkwood, *Celtis africana* – deciduous tree
Cape honeysuckle, *Tecomaria capensis* – scrambling shrub
Kaffirboom (lucky-bean tree), *Erythrina caffra* – deciduous tree.

Frost zone in Natal and eastern Cape
White pear, *Apodytes dimidiata* – evergreen tree
Natal bottlebrush, *Greyia sutherlandii* – deciduous tree
Cape fig, *Ficus capensis* – semi-deciduous tree
White stinkwood, *Celtis africana* – deciduous tree
Yellowwoods, *Podocarpus* species – evergreen trees
Wild dagga, *Leonotis leonurus* – shrub

Transvaal Highveld and Orange Free State
Wild olive, *Olea africana* – evergreen tree
Bloubos, *Diospyros lycioides* – evergreen tree or shrub
Kaffirboom, *Erythrina lysistemon* – deciduous tree
Cabbage tree, *Cussonia paniculata* – evergreen tree
Karree, *Rhus lancea* – evergreen tree

Winter rainfall region – south-western Cape
Proteas, *Protea* species – evergreen shrubs and trees
Ericas, *Erica* species – evergreen shrubs
Wild peach, *Kiggelaria africana* – evergreen tree
Tree fuschia, *Halleria lucida* – evergreen tree
Keurboom, *Virgilia oroboides* – evergreen tree

Finally, aloes and proteas grow in most areas and a variety of species is available to the gardener.

Many people derive pleasure from merely reading about Nature without ever really being a participant. Such armchair enthusiasts are not to be scorned, for undoubtedly some become most erudite. Nothing, however, can surpass the pleasure of actually being in the field, of seeing animals and flowers in their natural settings. Observation is, after all, the first and fundamental step towards understanding.

As with most pastimes, birding is one that can be even more stimulating if approached systematically and with a degree of discipline. The following notes are suggestions to help you to derive the greatest pleasure from watching birds.

A notebook and pencil are basic tools for birdwatching, useful for taking descriptions and making sketches of birds you have never seen before, or for making lists of the species seen in a day or in an area. Today, however, many bird-watchers have dispensed with notebooks and instead use mini tape-recorders. These have obvious advantages as a long series of observations can be taped in the field and then later transcribed into a book or even re-taped onto a larger master-tape and filed for easy retrieval.

The method of note-taking is, however, a secondary concern; more important is what to do when confronted with a new species. First, quickly note down the features that strike you immediately, for example the shape of the bill, the length of the legs, size of body in relation to tail, and any peculiar colour combinations. Try also to compare the bird with species familiar to you and, if possible, try to see the bird in different positions, postures and in flight. By building up a written or dictated description of the bird combined with rough sketches, you should have enough information to be able to use this or another bird book to make a correct identification. The accompanying picture of a ringed plover and an open wing, show the basic structure of a bird. Memorising the various parts of the anatomy as shown, will prove very useful when taking down a brief description. Finally, do remember to note as far as possible at the time, not only the bird's colour, shape and size, but also its behaviour, for another opportunity to observe it may be long in coming your way.

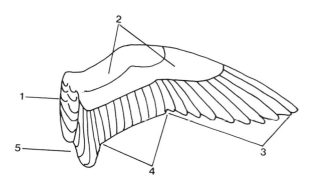

1. Scapulars 2. Wing Coverts 3. Primaries 4. Secondaries 5. Tertials

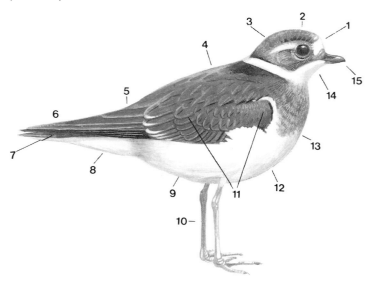

1. Forehead 2. Crown 3. Nape 4. Back 5. Rump 6. Primaries 7. Tail 8. Vent 9. Belly 10. Tarsus 11. Wing Coverts 12. Lower Breast 13. Breast 14. Throat 15. Bill

In addition to a notebook or tape-recorder, a pair of binoculars is about the only other essential piece of equipment for birdwatching. Granted, birds can be observed without binoculars, but few experiences are as frustrating as trying to identify a bird that is just beyond the power of the un-aided eye. The choice of binoculars is important. Two types are readily available: the standard prism and the more-recently-developed, roof-prism. The standard prism is less expensive and, therefore, the most commonly used. The huge variety of models and sizes available, however, can make the initial choice difficult. Points to consider are magnification, size of the object lens and field-of-view. Binoculars marked 7 x 40 indicate that the object being viewed is brought seven times closer, while '40' refers to the width of the object lens in millimetres. The size of the object lens combined with the magnification dictates field-of-view, literally the width of the image as seen through the lenses.

The field-of-view is all-important as this also determines the brightness of the image; generally, the higher the magnification, the smaller the field-of-view and the duller the image. Among birdwatchers, the most popular sizes in standard prism models are 7 x 40, 8 x 30, 9 x 35 and 10 x 50. The last, however, is not recommended, for binoculars with such lenses are large and cumbersome, difficult to hold still and tiresome to carry in the field for any length of time.

In the standard prism range any models costing less than R50 tend to be of poor quality, lack reasonable performance and are easily broken. Quality is assured with models bearing well-known names such as Carl Zeiss, Nikon and Yashica. These robust yet fine instruments are a delight to use and a pleasure to own. They will give endless hours of good performance without causing eye strain.

Roof-prism binoculars, with their complex system of small prisms, are much smaller and lighter. They are compact, easy to carry and usually offer exceptional performance as they have no external moving parts and are, therefore, completely dustproof. The best models are made by Carl Zeiss and Leitz and are priced at many hundreds of Rands.

In the past, hunters, trappers and naturalists used whistles which attracted birds by imitating their calls. Even today, in hunting and gun shops these duck and geese whistles can be purchased. Birdwatchers no longer equip themselves with such 'instruments'; instead, bird calls are played through small, hand-held tape-recorders to attract the more furtive species into the open. In thick reedbeds and forests many species are more often heard than seen, and in these habitats a tape-recorder becomes an indispensible tool. Using a small hand-held directional microphone the birder 'tapes' the hidden bird's song or call and then plays it back at an audible volume. The bird should then respond, literally by answering its own taped call, but believing it to be that of a competitor invading its territory. Curiosity, or indignation at the intrusion, may encourage it to move closer and closer to the source of the call and this is when the observer may obtain a good view of the otherwise secretive bird.

Not all species will respond to their taped calls, but all strange calls are worth recording and experimenting with. This technique will pay dividends, for soon the more familiar calls will be committed to memory and out of the previous 'confusion' of bird sounds, the more difficult ones will be easier to pin-point.

Taking photographs of birds is a pastime allied to conventional 'birding' and one that has gained much popularity, especially in recent years with the development of the 35-mm reflex camera. Cameras and lenses can be very expensive, but some are reasonably priced and within the means of most birders. Many books have been written on the techniques of bird and mammal photography and we suggest that you read one before purchasing the necessary equipment to capture birds on film. There are no cameras designed specifically for bird photography, but many models are suited to the purpose. Most professionals opt for the small, single-lens-reflex 35-mm camera which allows one to focus through the lens and to 'frame' immediately the intended subject. These cameras have the added advantage of having interchangeable lenses. Most bird species are too shy to photograph with a standard lens for, by the time the enthusiastic photographer has crashed his way close enough for a meaningful 'shot', the subject will have long gone.

Telephoto lenses which allow the photographer to keep his distance, but at the same time to fill his lens with the target bird, have therefore become indispensible. Recently, zoom lenses have become popular and a 200-400 mm zoom gives ideal flexibility for bird photography. Such long lenses can give superb results, but are sometimes difficult to manage. When using a telephoto or zoom lens remember that any movement is magnified and that the camera must be held very steady to prevent a blurred photograph. A tripod is very useful in this respect, but it may be cumbersome to carry. The window ledge of your car, too, is a suitable rest for a telephoto lens. The car itself makes a good hide, especially effective in game reserves, and allows close approach to many birds.

While correct identification of a species or the 'freezing' of a fine specimen on film are undeniably great pleasures, all birders should, in addition to seeing, try also to answer questions posed by the objects of their interest. For example, what makes the bird so colourful or so drab, why does a male appear to have many wives, why do so many birds perch prominently to sing thus making themselves obvious to predators? Such areas of behaviourism have been touched upon in this introduction and in the following chapters, and there are many excellent works devoted solely to the subject. It is, however, a vast and only partially-understood field of study and any birder will be richly-rewarded by his efforts not only to see but also to understand.

This short introduction should give a basic idea of some of the elements of birdwatching in South Africa. There are obviously many other facets to the hobby and should you be interested, you may care to join the Southern African Ornithological Society, P.O. Box 87234, Houghton, Johannesburg 2041. The Society has branches centered in most cities and membership will entitle you to share in their publications, outings, lectures and film shows.

TOWNS, CITIES AND GARDENS

In building towns and cities, man has dramatically changed the South African environment. For instance, where Johannesburg stands today, little over a century ago there was nothing but typical African grassland. These great changes, particularly our increasing pollution and the disturbance we cause, have proved hostile to many birds. Yet, some species have not only adapted to living closely with us, but have also become dependent on our refuse for food and on the artificially stable environments of our gardens and parks for their survival. The city centres have hoards of pigeons, starlings and sparrows. Lanner falcons have been attracted in turn to prey on other bird species and they can be seen even nesting on the ledges of buildings. In this chapter all the birds shown occur in South African urban areas, sometimes in surprising abundance.

Ironically, in ridding ourselves of organic wastes we have created a particularly rich habitat for birds. If your town or city has a sewage farm, visit it. The odours may be unpleasant, but the filtration beds and surrounding vegetation hold numerous birds, including rare and vagrant species. A few cities have created bird sanctuaries and three of

Crowned Plover

Feral Pigeon

special note are the Austin Roberts Sanctuary in Pretoria, the Rondevlei Sanctuary in Cape Town and the Beechwood Mangroves of the Umgeni estuary in Durban. Some sanctuaries have special hides for enthusiasts and these not only provide opportunities for close viewing of the varied bird-life, but also excellent opportunities for photography.

Crowned Plover *(Vanellus coronatus)*. This large long-legged wading bird has adapted well to suburbia where it frequents and breeds on well-watered sports fields and other wide open grassy areas. It is known locally as the 'Kieweet' — a good rendition of its call which is often heard at night. The black crown narrowly-bordered with white, as well as the white belly and long red legs, distinguish this species from other plovers and in flight, large white wing patches are revealed. When disturbed, especially during the breeding season if eggs or young are threatened, the birds will swoop around the intruder screeching their 'Kieweet' cry in loud and noisy protest. Virtually no nest is made, the eggs being laid in a shallow scrape in the ground and relying on their mottled camouflage for protection.

Feral Pigeon *(Columba livia)*. Since the time of the ancient Egyptians, pigeons have been domesticated and conditioned to convey messages attached to their legs. For many years, too, these birds have been kept by countless devotees of pigeon racing and it is from this source that the majority of city pigeons originally came. The feral pigeon's ancestor, the rock pigeon, still lives in the wild state in Europe and Asia and many city pigeons show the true plumage of the wild bird — an overall grey, with black bars on the wings and a small white patch on the rump which is visible during flight. More often, however, feral pigeons exhibit so many permutations of these colours that it is impossible to describe them all here. Breeding occurs throughout the year and the ledges and sills of tall city buildings provide ideal nesting sites. City dwellers have actively encouraged the settlement of these and other pigeon and dove species by putting out grain and bread crumbs for them. In some cities, street vendors sell seeds and nuts especially for people to 'feed the birds'.

Rock Pigeon *(Columba guinea)*. This pigeon has moved, in significant numbers, from its former habitat of craggy cliffs and mountains, to inhabit towns and cities where it lives alongside the feral pigeon with which it is thought to occasionally interbreed. The reasons for this habitat expansion are uncertain, but could include the fact that tall and high-rise buildings with ample nooks and ledges for nesting, superficially resemble the rock faces of their natural environment. The chestnut back, white-speckled wings and blue-grey rump are characteristic and at close range a reddish-coloured, unfeathered patch of skin is visible around the eyes. When drinking, most birds scoop up water in their lower beaks and then swallow by lifting their bills upwards, allowing the water to flow down their throats. All doves and pigeons, however, have the ability to drink directly by suction and are, therefore, able to take in rapidly, large volumes of water.

Red-eyed Turtle Dove *(Streptopelia semitorquata)*. Though very like the Cape turtle dove, this species is larger, more heavily built, has a darker body colour and a pale grey bar across the end of the upper surface of the tail. The characteristic red eye, however, is difficult to see except at close range. This pigeon is less city-bound than many doves and prefers the denser vegetation of garden environments. The nest is a flimsy platform in trees, and is often so loosely constructed that eggs can sometimes be seen from below. The young are fed for the first few days after hatching on 'pigeon milk', a highly nutritious curd-like substance manufactured by cells in the crops of both parents and which is similar in composition to mammalian milk. To receive the regurgitated milk, the young thrust their heads into the parent's throat. Milk-feeding in birds is peculiar to the pigeon and dove family.

Laughing Dove *(Streptopelia senegalensis)*. In many parts of the world, the scarcity of doves has led to considerable sums being spent on stocking public gardens and parks with ornamental fantail and Barbary doves. South Africa is fortunate, therefore, in having an abundance of indigenous doves in its cities, towns and gardens. Of these the laughing dove is certainly the most familiar. It shows little fear of man and can be seen strutting confidently around city pavements, garden paths and parks. The laughing dove is one of the smaller species in South Africa and is easily identified by the freckled necklace which extends round the sides of the neck and the breast, but it lacks the black hind collar of similar species. The soft bubbling call-note, reminiscent of someone chuckling, gives this dove its name. During courtship displays, males rise steeply into the air, descending slowly with spread wings and the fanned tail showing its conspicuous white sides.

Rock Pigeon

Red-eyed Turtle Dove

Laughing Dove

Speckled Mousebird *(Colius striatus)*. The mousebird family is only found in Africa and the name aptly reflects both the habit of creeping and crawling mouse-like through tangled vegetation, and the short, hairy, belly feathers common to all mousebirds. As the speckled markings on the plumage are often very difficult to discern, this species is best distinguished from other, more striking, members of the family by its black face and bill and the lack of distinctive colours. Speckled mousebirds are normally seen in flocks of as many as 12 or more birds and at night they huddle together, presumably to conserve heat. Their sociability may also help them in other ways. Information concerning the whereabouts of fruit-laden trees, for example, may be exchanged between flock members by means of a continual, squeaky, contact call. Breeding starts in early summer and the nest is a scruffy cup of twigs placed in a tree or shrub. Three or four eggs are laid and the young start to clamber around the nest tree well before they can fly.

Red-faced Mousebird *(Colius indicus)*. Though similar to the speckled mousebird, the bright red base to the bill and red feet and legs are characteristic. The red-faced mousebird is also more powerful on the wing and flies long distances strongly and directly, with rapid wing beats interspersed with short glides. The call is a very distinctive 'vee vee vee' and is exchanged between members of small parties in flight. Like other mousebirds this species spends many hours each day clambering from branch to branch and feed-

Red-faced Mousebird

Speckled Mousebird

Little Bee-eater

Brown-hooded Kingfisher

ing rapaciously on fruit and berries, a habit which makes it very unpopular with many farmers and gardeners.

Brown-hooded Kingfisher *(Halcyon albiventris)*. This species is one of several kingfishers that does not eat fish – the name though, quite correctly reflects the close relationship to its fish-eating kin. Diet consists largely of insects, but occasionally small reptiles, birds or mammals are also taken. In typical kingfisher fashion, this species keeps a sharp look-out from a high perch and when suitable prey comes within range it swoops down to snatch the animal in its beak. Kingfishers are brightly-coloured and though a perched brown-hooded kingfisher looks somewhat drab, its flight reveals a bright flash of blue on the wings, rump and tail. The nest is placed in a chamber at the end of a burrow excavated in a steeply-sloping bank and the eggs, in common with most

hole-nesting birds, are white instead of being coloured. This is quite logical as an egg placed in a dark chamber needs no camouflage and has no need for pigment in the eggshell.

Little Bee-eater *(Melittophagus pusillus)*. Though the smallest bee-eater in South Africa, this species is one of the most delicately coloured. The yellow throat, combined with a black crescent-shaped collar, and orange breast and belly, distinguishes it from all other members of the family. It prefers perches near the ground from where it launches attacks on flying insects, and after these sorties it usually returns to the same point. In the low-level greenery of its habitat its like-coloured back blends well, often making it difficult to spot, especially when it sits motionless. The nest is placed at the end of a tunnel which is excavated low down on a bank or slight mound in sandy soil.

Hoopoe *(Upupa epops)*. The striking black and white wing pattern and long cockatoo-type crest are unmistakeable. This crest is only raised and fanned, however, when the bird is alarmed or when it alights. Both the common and scientific names reflect its call which consists of variations on 'hoop hoop hoo hoo'. The long downward-curving bill is well suited to its purpose of probing for worms, grubs and other insects. The nest is made either in a hole in the ground, a crevice among rocks or in the cleft of a branch and is a particularly messy and smelly abode. So unpleasant is the odour and general state of the nest, that it is thought by some to deter potential predators.

Pied Barbet *(Lybius leucomelas)*. The single, harsh, nasal call note and low-pitched 'hoop hoop hoop' are the most frequent sounds from this species, but occasionally a nasal 'cheeh cheeh' is also heard. Its colours are distinctive – it is the only barbet to have whitish underparts with a black bib and breast. Barbets are related to woodpeckers and like them, excavate nest holes in dead tree trunks or branches, using their exceptionally strong bills to chip out the wood. The name barbet comes from the tuft of feathers and bristles at the base of the bill.

Little Swift *(Apus affinis)*. This is another species that has adapted successfully to cities and towns where tall granary towers and buildings provide ideal breeding localities. Like most swifts, these little birds only settle on level ground when forced to. This is understandable as they are particularly vulnerable when grounded, their relatively short legs and long wings making take-off difficult. The little swift's broad white rump and squared-ended tail, not forked as with other species, are clearly visible, even when the bird circles high above the ground. Though a migratory species and a summer visitor to South Africa, a few records do exist of this species being spotted in winter.

Pied Crow *(Corvus albus)*. Though ungainly on the ground where it hops and sidles around picking up food, in flight the pied crow can perform some spectacular aerial manoeuvres. The white belly rules out confusion with any other crow in South Africa. During the spring and early summer breeding season the pied crow is usually seen singly or in pairs, but in the non-breeding season large flocks gather in the evenings to roost in tall trees, sometimes in the centre of a city. Large untidy stick nests are built, frequently on top of telegraph poles or pylons. The pied crow is an opportunistic and omnivorous feeder and it does well on human garbage, especially where crowds congregate such as at drive-in restaurants and theatres, racecourses and sports stadiums. It has also become a popular pet in many households and, being a good mimic, can be taught to imitate the human voice. In rural areas the pied crow is much maligned as a 'killer' of young or weak stock, but this reputation is exaggerated and any damage to farm animals that may occur is far outweighed by its eating of crop-destroying insects.

Black-collared Barbet *(Lybius torquatus)*. This species is larger than the pied barbet and is very striking with its crimson face and blue-black collar. The black-collared barbet is usually seen in pairs flitting in and out of trees and bushes in search of berries and fruit. Pairs have a comical duetting display in which both birds sit together on a branch and one sways and bobs calling 'doo' whilst its mate calls 'doodle'. The 'doo' is higher-pitched than the 'doodle' call and these are repeated very rapidly 6–8 times, the last few notes trailing off. Duetting is thought to reinforce the bond between pairs and in this species is sometimes a prelude to copulation. This species also excavates a nest hole in trees, using its powerful bill to chip away the wood.

Hoopoe

Pied Barbet

Little Swift

Pied Crow

Black-collared Barbet

Olive Thrush

Cape Robin

Black-eyed Bulbul

Cape Bulbul

Olive Thrush *(Turdus olivaceus).* Though usually favouring the dense undergrowth of forests, the olive thrush, like the Cape robin, has adapted well to the gardens and parks of suburbia. When feeding, it runs or hops along the ground, stopping suddenly to cock its head to one side to listen for the worms on which it feeds. Snails are also favoured and the shells are broken open by bashing them against a rock. These 'thrush anvils' can be recognized by the piles of broken shells strewn about them. This bird can be identified by its orange bill, speckled throat, olive-brown back, wings and tail and the orange wash on its belly and flanks.

Cape Robin *(Cossypha caffra).* Though typically a very shy furtive bird that keeps well hidden in thick tangles of vegetation, in some parts of South Africa the Cape robin has adapted well to garden living and has become quite confiding, feeding openly on insects on lawns and garden vegetation. Many urban gardens, especially those rich in insect life and well planted with indigenous plants, could, in fact, appear to the Cape robin as mere extensions of its natural habitat. Like most robins in South Africa, the sides of the tail, in both males and females, have bright orange-chestnut markings which are very conspicuous when the tail is well cocked and possibly serve as a signalling system to other members of the species. The orange throat colour which extends on to the breast, the black eye patches and the white stripe above the eyes all help to identify this bird.

Black-eyed Bulbul *(Pycnonotus barbatus).* Though visually very similar to the Cape bulbul, this species has a paler breast and lacks white eye wattles. It is a common and conspicuous resident of Natal, Zululand and much of the Transvaal. It is also a strongly territorial bird and is very noisy and aggressive. It will, without fear or hesitation, even mob cats or snakes threatening its nest or territory. Though not a gregarious species, the scolding calls of a pair of black-eyed bulbuls will invariably attract other bulbuls as well as other species and the expulsion of a common enemy seems a community affair. The black-eyed bulbul feeds busily on flowers, especially *Aloe* species, when the forehead and bill become covered in yellow pollen. As it moves from plant to plant feeding, this bird, as with many others, undoubtedly fulfils an extremely important role in cross-pollination.

Cape Bulbul *(Pycnonotus capensis).* This endemic species is confined to the winter rainfall areas of the southern Cape. Though similar to its eastern cousin, the black-eyed bulbul, it is shyer and is distinguished by its darker body colouration and conspicuous white eye wattles. Both the Cape bulbul and the black-eyed bulbul show a bright yellow vent. The Cape bulbul is usually seen in pairs which are believed to remain together for life and with the onset of spring, flimsy eye-level nests of twigs and fine roots are constructed in bushes, especially Port Jackson willows. Diet is varied – fruit and berries are preferred, though like flycatchers they often swoop low over grass in pursuit of insects.

European Starling

Indian Mynah

Cape Wagtail

European Starling (*Sturnus vulgaris*). Since its introduction to Cape Town by Cecil Rhodes in 1899 this bird has, like the house sparrow, established itself as a permanent member of urban society. It has become exceptionally common in the Cape Province, so numerous in some areas as to be considered a pest, and causes great damage especially in vineyards. This remarkable success in the western Cape may be attributed to the lack of an effective competitor in the region. It is doubtful whether it would have enjoyed the same measure of success in Natal, however, where the mynah, also an import, has filled a similar niche. From a distance this species appears black overall with a yellow bill, but at closer range the plumage is bright with subtle hues of metallic purples and greens and with small white flecks on the belly and back. The starling is an accomplished song mimic and from an exposed perch it bubbles and chirps, all the while flicking its wings, bill pointing skywards and long throat hackles vibrating with the noise.

Indian Mynah (*Acridotheres tristis*). This handsome bird is easily recognized by the yellow beak and mask, white patches on the wings and the white-tipped, rounded tail. It was originally introduced to Durban from India at the turn of the century and though it is not known how many birds were originally released, with no competition from indigenous species, the mynah was quick to make itself at home in the growing port. So successful were they in their adopted habitat that, with the development of town and cities, they soon spread inland. Today they are well established as far as Johannesburg and Pretoria, and are so numerous that they are considered by some to be obnoxious pests. Mynahs may remain with the same mate throughout life and pairs and family parties can be seen running and hopping around gardens and open grassy areas, continually probing for grubs and worms. Fruit and kitchen scraps supplement the diet of this omnivorous bird. In the evenings large numbers gather in trees to roost and set up a cacophony of screeches and chirps.

Cape Wagtail (*Motacilla capensis*). Open grassy and sunny gardens are extensions of the Cape wagtail's natural environment and are favourite haunts of this engaging little bird. It is frequently seen as it dashes comically to and fro, stopping only momentarily to peck at insects in the grass, its tail bobbing up and down as it teeters on long legs. This continual tail-wagging is very characteristic and the dun grey back and black breast band help to prevent confusion with its closer relatives. Pairs or small family parties are most common, but communal roosting also occurs, with large numbers sometimes gathering in trees in city centres. Nesting sites vary widely, but are more often near water where a small deeply cupped nest is normally placed well out of view.

Fiscal Shrike (*Lanius collaris*). This species is also known locally as the Jackie Hangman or butcherbird, both apt in view of its seemingly-gruesome habit of impaling prey, sometimes alive, on thorns or barbed wire. In this manner fiscal shrikes often build up 'larders', supposedly to tide them over when food is scarce. Though insects and small lizards make up the bulk of the diet, this species has also been known to kill small birds and mammals. Its wide distribution, contrasting colours and habit of sitting on an exposed perch while keeping a sharp look out for possible prey make the fiscal shrike one of the most familiar species in South Africa.

Fiscal Shrike

Cape White-eye *(Zosterops pallidus)*. A thin circle of white feathers around the eyes gives this bird its name, the real eye colour being dark brown. The Cape white-eye is an active little bird and behaves very much like a small warbler, always on the move creeping through foliage in search of caterpillars and other insects. Fruit is also favoured and, as the photograph suggests, figs are very popular. White-eyes almost always congregate in small parties of 4–6, continually calling a thin 'seep treep'. These contact calls are uttered by many birds and are quite separate from their songs. Their true meaning is not fully understood, but probably they serve to keep the members of the group in touch with one another, especially in thick greenery where sight contact is difficult. Calls of this nature could also function to communicate food sources or even to warn of danger. The small, deeply cupped nest is slung beneath a slender forked branch, normally on the outer fringes of a tree or bush.

House Sparrow *(Passer domesticus)*. For centuries, human settlements have provided the house sparrow with ideal nesting sites in roofs, gutters and walls, as well as a steady supply of food, from kitchen scraps and spilled grain to the seed of garden grass. This has brought about an almost total dependence on man for survival. Not surprisingly, therefore, the distribution of this species has matched that of European man. It came to South Africa via India and from England and since its introduction to South Africa, initially to Durban and later to the Cape, this tiny bird has spread rapidly. In recent years the process has accelerated and the house sparrow has even established itself in the remotest areas including islands off the western Cape coast. The male, shown here, is easily distinguished from all other sparrows in South Africa as it has a grey forehead and crown, chestnut back and black bib. Females and young are dowdy and nondescript but have a small pale bar on the wings. The house sparrow is gregarious and communities are found in and around isolated farms to towns and cities, their untidy nests occupying any available crevice or hole in buildings.

Cape Sparrow *(Passer melanurus)*. This endemic species occurred in its natural environment well before the arrival of settlers from Europe and has not developed the same degree of dependence as the house sparrow. Though common in towns and cities, the Cape sparrow is still frequently seen in flocks far from urban development. It also usually prefers a much drier habitat. Males are unmistakeable with their striking black and white head patterns, whereas females resemble their house sparrow counterparts, but are larger and more robust with brighter chestnut backs. The Cape sparrow has not been slow to take advantage of the opportunities of shelter and food that urban development offers. This often leads it into direct conflict with its imported relative, for where the Cape and the house sparrow frequent the same territory, fierce competition arises over nest sites and available food – an unequal rivalry as the Cape sparrow, being the larger and more aggressive bird, normally wins. Nests are large, untidy, round bundles of grasses, twigs and feathers, usually placed in trees and bushes and less frequently in holes and crevices in buildings.

Cape White-eye

House Sparrow

Cape Sparrow

GRASSLANDS AND CULTIVATION

South Africa is a land of wide open veld, of acacia-dotted grasslands which stretch endlessly before the eyes. But South Africa is also farming country and great tracts of land have been altered by the machinery of modern agriculture and given over to revenue-earning crops. Though the extent of grasslands has been reduced by cultivation, the considerable areas remaining have been altered little by man's activities except where overgrazing by livestock has stretch-ed the veld's recuperative powers. Whereas the plant species of unspoiled grasslands are many and varied and largely indigenous, croplands are, by contrast, completely novel and artificial, with the plants being introduced from overseas and cultivated fields making monotonously uniform environments. The heavy fertilization of soil which goes hand in hand with large-scale cultivation, however, probably helps to stimulate plant growth on field verges and this provides food and nesting places which have attracted a number of birds. In general, the birds that have adapted to life alongside or in cultivated fields tend to be very common, with a great density of a few species.

To the birdwatcher, grassland birds can be a constant irritation as most are dull-coloured and many lack distinctive marks which would distinguish them from a host of other 'little brown jobs'. Some of the pipits and cisticolas, for instance, can only be recognized by their calls and displays. Furthermore, the birds of the veld are often difficult even to see, let alone identify. Their drab colours blend well with their surroundings and many bury themselves in the grass, or run behind a convenient tuft just as a good viewing position is reached.

The inconspicuous plumages of these birds have obvious advantages, but there are drawbacks as well, as it is difficult for males to advertise themselves and their territories to potential mates or neighbours. During the breeding season, therefore, many perch on raised vantage points, have characteristic courtship calls, or make conspicuous display flights, high above the ground. It is at these times that the birdwatcher stands the best chance of telling views.

It is difficult to pin-point the best birding areas since the high plateau regions of the Transvaal and Orange Free State are so vast and virtually any grassland that has not been overgrazed and has solid stands of 'rooigras' (*Themeda triandra*) should hold a good sprinkling of birds. There are also several game reserves on the highveld with carefully managed grasslands and these provide very good birding opportunities.

Black-headed Heron (*Ardea melanocephala*). Herons and egrets are closely related, and the cattle egret and this heron are the only members of a normally aquatic family that feed away from water. Both species, however, join others in mixed heronries to breed and roost alongside waterways. Black-headed herons forage for food as they walk steadily through grasslands or fields, every now and then darting forward rapidly to grab locusts, lizards and mice in their sharp bills. They even take on snakes, including the fast-striking puffadder, and have been observed getting the better of these poisonous reptiles by crushing them with the tip of the bill. Adult black-headed herons stand more than a metre tall and though like most herons they have an overall grey plumage, the crown and hind region of the neck is conspicuously black. In young birds the same areas are pale grey.

Cattle Egret (*Bubulcus ibis*). Cattle egrets are a common sight wherever cattle are grazing and as such are familiar to most people. Though popularly known as 'tick birds' they rarely eat these parasites and instead feed voraciously on vast numbers of grasshoppers and other insects that are disturbed by cattle as they browse in the veld. The bright white plumage of cattle egrets is similar to that of great white, yellow-billed and little egrets, but confusion is unlikely in the open veld as these related species seldom wander from wetlands. Cattle egrets, like black-headed herons, always forage away from water, but usually return to their waterside roosts or nests in trees and reedbeds where they often form dense colonies with as many as several hundred birds grouped into one small area. Visitors to the Austin Roberts Sanctuary in Pretoria will be able to observe such a colony at close range, and to note during the breeding season, the bright red bills and legs of these egrets which at other times are yellowish.

White Stork (*Ciconia ciconia*). This summer visitor to South Africa from Europe is the fabled bird that brings babies, but this myth is easily dispelled as the fast-declining numbers of storks could not possibly keep up with the exploding human population! White storks feed predominantly on insects and often follow swarms of locusts. The chemical control of these swarms is a direct cause of diminishing stork populations, for though pesticides are no longer used to any great extent in Europe, the birds still accumulate large residues of poison from the massive crop-spraying programmes common in Africa. White storks are of obvious value to farmers and South African agriculturists should attempt to match the efforts of their European counterparts by reducing the pesticide load that these birds carry out of Africa each year. White storks breed during the summer in central Europe where their large nests often adorn tall church steeples. The residents of many small towns identify strongly with these great white birds and make sure that adequate nesting platforms are always available.

Secretary Bird (*Sagittarius serpentarius*). An upright carriage and a stately pace characterize these elegant birds as they stride through the veld on their long, stilt-like legs. These spindly, seemingly-fragile limbs are deceptive, as they not only provide an obvious height advantage while hunting in tall grass, but are also effective weapons, for the secretary bird packs a kick like a mule and with a few, well-directed blows can immobilize birds the size of francolins, mammals as large as hares, and good-sized snakes. Secretary birds form pairs and their nests are large platform structures placed on top of low trees and may, in fact, cover the entire canopy. Several young are reared at a time and the resultant demand for food is great. Parents therefore spend much of the day walking to and from the nest as they hunt and deliver food for their ever-hungry young. Though secretary birds spend most of their time on the ground, they are strong fliers and as this bird demonstrates, they have an impressive wingspan. On hot days they are often seen riding thermals high above the veld, their long legs and central tail feathers trailing behind.

Black-headed Heron

Secretary Bird

Cattle Egret

White Stork

27

Black-shouldered Kite

Swainson's Francolin

Helmeted Guinea-fowl

Black-shouldered Kite *(Elanus caeruleus).* These raptors are very common and conspicuous in cultivated areas where they often perch on telephone poles and power pylons, their white breasts resembling ceramic insulators. From these vantage points, or while hovering, they survey the ground below for mice and rats. On sighting prey they drop out of the sky, feet first, their speed of descent being controlled by the angle of the wings which are extended upwards like a parachute. Black-shouldered kites move around nomadically in search of the best feeding areas and, where rodents are particularly abundant, great numbers of these birds may accumulate in small areas. During times of plenty, breeding may also occur irrespective of the time of year and several broods may be raised in succession. When less food is available, however, communal roosts are formed which probably serve as information centres concerning regions of greater promise. Adults are about 350 mm long and have piercing red eyes, but these are visible only at close range.

Swainson's Francolin *(Francolinus swainsonii).* This species is essentially a bird of the thornveld that has adapted to cultivated areas. This change has been so successful that today the species is far more numerous than it was previously in the smaller areas of its former habitat. Adult Swainson's francolins stand about 300 mm tall and male birds have spurs which are clearly visible on this beady-eyed specimen perched atop a termite mound. In the early morning and late afternoon, males often take up position on any such raised perch and call endlessly — the need to advertise their presence to competitors, as well as their sexual prowess to prospective mates, obviously being greater than the threat from potential predators. Females are less boisterous and spend all their time on the ground, where they search and scratch for insects and seeds. Francolins are popular table birds, though their desirability in this respect probably has more to do with the elitist concept of eating 'game birds' than with the actual qualities of their flesh.

Helmeted Guinea-fowl *(Numida meleagris).* The helmeted guinea-fowl shown here at a watering-hole display typical flock behaviour, with some of the birds drinking while those on the outer edge keep a wary eye out for possible danger. Large flocks like this gather during the non-breeding season and keep close together during the day while at night they roost well-protected in large trees. In areas where trees have been levelled to make way for croplands these birds have taken to roosting on power pylons and it is not uncommon for them to be electrocuted. Breeding takes place during the summer months when pairs or small family groups are more common. Like Swainson's francolins, helmeted guinea-fowl have adapted successfully to cultivated areas where they are now very common and favoured game birds. As they feed mainly on seed and insects, both of which are pecked from the ground, it is not surprising that they have exploited the ready food supply provided by these heavily fertilized regions.

Blue Crane

Crowned Crane

Crowned Crane (*Balearica regulorum*). The spectacular crowned crane is certainly the most colourful of the three crane species in South Africa, the other two being the blue crane and the rare wattled crane which is now endangered in this country. The crowned crane favours marshy areas for breeding, but at other times pairs or even large flocks move out into open grassland and cultivated farmlands to forage for food. These feeding parties sometimes damage recently-planted crops, but even the most unforgiving farmers must agree that their beauty offers substantial compensation for the occasional damage caused. At night crowned cranes gather in large flocks along waterways. Their call is most distinctive and aptly described by the Afrikaans name *mahem,* or perhaps, a nasal 'arhum'. Courtship dances are colourful and energetic with both the male and the female prancing around and leaping into the air with spread wings.

Black Korhaan

Blacksmith Plover

Cape Dikkop

Blue Crane (*Anthropoides paradisea*). The blue crane is the national bird of South Africa, and it would be difficult indeed to choose a more graceful and elegant bird for the role. It is also depicted on our five cent coin. The species is common in South Africa and a few neighbouring states, but is not found anywhere else in the world. As seed eaters, blue cranes are commonly seen foraging in pairs, small groups or even large flocks. It is natural, therefore, that many have been attracted by the bountiful food supply of croplands, and in some areas they anger farmers by plundering recently-planted fields. They do, however, also benefit agriculture as the seeds and seedlings of weeds are attacked with equal voracity. The long, flowing plumes that drape near the tail are in fact elongate wing feathers and these are shown to good effect during courtship rituals when birds of both sexes jump around with their wings spread in display.

Black Korhaan (*Eupodotis afra*). This species is common throughout much of the Transvaal and Orange Free State highveld as well as the dry Karoo scrub of the Cape. Adult males, like the one shown here, are striking birds. Their conspicuous, noisy display flights across the open veld are unmistakeable and they can attract attention at a range of one or two kilometres with their harsh 'karackaracka . . .' calls. Females and immature birds are duller and lack the distinctive black head and neck of the males. They are also more secretive and therefore far more difficult to spot. Nests are simple scrapes in the ground and one or two brownish-olive eggs are laid which, unlike the oval eggs of most birds, are almost round.

Blacksmith Plover (*Vanellus armatus*). In many areas of South Africa blacksmith plovers are commonly seen strutting around the edges of open water, but they do also spend a lot of time in open grassland where they forage for small insects. Adult birds stand some 25 cm tall and their wholly black and white plumage is distinctive; other plover species in South Africa have various areas of brown feathering. Blacksmith plovers have characteristic 'tink .. tink .. tink ..' calls, reminiscent of a blacksmith hammering away at his anvil. Nests are small scrapes in the ground near water. Breeding pairs protect their nest and young vigorously and become very aggressive at the approach of any intruder. They are undaunted by the size of the trespasser and fly up calling harshly, fearlessly dive-bombing even humans in an attempt to warn them off. Young birds leave the nest soon after hatching, but are very difficult to spot as they lie quite still in the undergrowth once the parents have given their alarm calls.

Cape Dikkop (*Burhinus capensis*). Dikkops spend much of the day resting quietly in the shade of a bush or among rocks where the birdwatcher is most likely to see them. They are unobtrusive birds and will quietly walk away from approaching intruders, the brown, speckled plumage helping to conceal their presence. At night, however, they become much more vociferous and their loud, shrill, contact whistles rend the air as they wing their way through the darkness. Dikkops have large eyes which suggest the good nocturnal vision necessary to hunt small insect prey. Nests are mere scrapes in the ground and are usually sited in shade. The two heavily-spotted, brown eggs take about 25 days to hatch and the precocious young are able to walk and feed themselves immediately. The closely-related water dikkop is very similar, but this species never strays from water and is distinguished by the pale bar on its wings which contrasts with the brown, speckled wings of the Cape dikkop.

European Swallow

Rufous-naped Lark

Red-capped Lark

Rufous-naped Lark (*Mirafra africana*). This lark is relatively easy to identify on the wing as it shows obvious, russet patches on the flight feathers. When perched on fence posts, bushes or termite mounds, it displays a slightly raised crest. From such perches the very distinctive double whistles, 'towee teeyou' are called, and these are probably the most characteristic sounds of the grasslands. For most of the time, however, the lark scurries along the ground seeking insects amongst the grass. It is amazingly fast and often disappears into a stand of grass, only to re-emerge within moments, several metres further on. Nests are cup-like structures tucked beneath tufts of grass, and two or three pinkish, speckled eggs are laid.

Red-capped Lark (*Calandrella cinerea*). Most bird species have distinctive and specific plumage patterns, but some show considerable variations, usually in colour intensity, between populations from different areas. This is often so with ground-dwelling grassland birds where plumage tends to match the soil colour of particular habitats. The attractive red-capped lark provides a good example of this phenomenon. It is one of the most colourful larks and the red-

brown cap and shoulder patches, clearly shown here, are more often than not sufficient to make a positive identification. There can, however, be a substantial and sometimes confusing variation in the basic brown colour of this species; in some regions, such as the Transvaal, plumage matches the rich red soils, but where the ground is pale or sandy it becomes almost beige. While capable of a fair running speed, the red-capped lark spends much of its time strutting about, busily searching for insects and seeds.

European Swallow (*Hirundo rustica*). This migrant from Europe and Asia arrives in September and October, and during the summer is the most abundant swallow in South Africa. An extensive trapping and ringing project on this species has shown that populations tend to ply between the same regions year after year; the birds which visit the eastern part of the country come mostly from Russia, while the majority of those in the Cape arrive from western Europe. Each evening great numbers of swallows gather from their wide-ranging daily patrols to roost communally in reed-beds. Though a few individual over-winter in the southern Cape, most head northwards in March, but before migrating,

Banded Sand Martin

Cliff Swallow

thousands muster, excitedly calling 'vitt . . . vitt . . . vitt' as they perch shoulder to shoulder along telephone wires. The brick-red throat, separated from the creamy white belly by a black collar, distinguishes this swallow from all others visiting South Africa. Juveniles, however, have white throats.

Cliff Swallow (Hirundo spilodera). These birds breed in colonies, with up to several hundred tightly-packed nests often tucked under a bridge or the eaves of a building, both of which provide suitable alternatives to rocky overhangs on cliff faces. Cliff swallows spend much of the early morning and late afternoon whirling around their colonies — often swinging right up to the nest, but at the last moment veering away. At other times they streak low over the grasslands as they pick insects out of the air. Though it is often difficult to get good views of these swallows during their fast erratic flights, the creamy-coloured upper rump and speckled upper breast are distinctive. Like the previous species, cliff swallows leave South Africa each autumn, but instead of undertaking the arduous trek to northern Europe, these birds spend the winter relatively near by in equatorial Africa.

Banded Sand Martin (Riparia cincta). Martins and swallows belong to the same family and are frequently confused, the differences between them being seldom clear. Similarities include size, long, pointed wings, tiny feet, and short, flattened bills. They also share the same fast, erratic flight and both groups feed wholly on minute insects caught in the air. In South Africa, however, most martins have brown plumages, while swallows tend to be predominantly glossy blue. The banded sand martin is a common grassland bird which is usually seen quartering the veld or hawking after insects just above the grass. At other times it will perch on a fence, with its brown breast band and white throat prominently displayed. The nest is a rounded chamber at the rear of a tunnel excavated into a steep bank and three or four pale eggs are laid in a small nest cup of fine grass. Newly-hatched nestlings frequently take position at the tunnel entrance where they perch with their bright orange mouths agape as a signal of an almost unceasing hunger which parent birds are hard-pushed to satisfy. After three weeks the young birds already resemble their parents and are able to join them on the wing.

Black Crow

Capped Wheatear

Stone Chat

Ant-eating Chat

Black Crow *(Corvus capensis).* This crow is completely black and as such is distinct from all the others in South Africa. It is a conspicuous resident of grasslands and is usually seen in pairs, flying across open country. Nests are normally placed in trees, but with telegraph poles and power pylons forming endless chains across the veld, the opportunistic black crow has taken full advantage of these artificial alternatives to breed away from woodland areas. A further example of this bird's successful adaptation to man's intrusion is that it has been quick to learn that bits of cast-off wire woven into the sturdy twig platform give added rigidity to the structure. Wool and other soft materials are used to line the nest. Eggs are pinkish brown as opposed to the blue-green eggs of most other crows.

Capped Wheatear *(Oenanthe pileata).* Seen from behind this bird is rather drab and has few distinctive marks or colours, but viewed head-on a striking, broad black breast-band is revealed which distinguishes the species from all other chats in South Africa. The bird here is about to enter its nest hole carrying a beakful of insects for its eagerly awaiting nestlings. The capped wheatear usually nests deep within a rodent burrow some distance from the surface and it is a wonder that this species ever breeds successfully as nests are not only exposed to flooding, but are also easily accessible to snake and rodent predators. The capped wheatear is normally seen perched on a termite mound and looks much like a shepherd surveying his flock; hence the Afrikaans name *skaapwagter.*

Stone Chat *(Saxicola torquata).* This species ranges through much of Africa and Europe as well as Asia. The male stone chat (shown here) is one of the brightest of the grassland birds. Females and young birds, however, are duller with pale brown fronts. These sparrow-sized chats frequently perch on fencing strands or telephone lines and this is where the birder is most likely to spot them. Stone chats are entirely insectivorous and from their raised perches they scan the air and ground below them for possible prey. On sighting a suitable meal they dart down to capture it on or just above the ground. Stone chats prefer temperate conditions and often migrate to higher, cooler, country for the summer breeding season and return to warmer regions in winter. Their neat, cup-like nests of twigs and grass are lined with feathery and other soft material and are usually placed well hidden near the ground. The eggs are bluish with red speckling and hatch after 14 or 15 days. Some 15 to 16 days later the young stone chats are ready to leave the nest.

Ant-eating Chat *(Myrmecocichla formicivora).* The ant-eating chat shown here stands typically upright on a tuft of grass. These dark brown birds are more commonly seen, however, when they perch like little sentinels atop the fence and telegraph poles lining roads through the highveld grasslands. From these or other vantage-points such as the crests of ant-hills, they make frequent, short, fluttering sorties and either return to their perches or drop to the ground to forage for insects and other small anthropods which, as for other chats, exclusively make up the diet. Bright white 'windows' on the undersides of the wings draw immediate attention to these birds in flight and make identification easy for no other dark brown bird in South Africa has these distinctive markings. White shoulder-flashes are obvious in some specimens when perched, but these are not shown by this sub-adult. During the summer breeding season ant-eating chats nest in holes in the ground, but unlike the capped wheatear, this species may excavate its own burrow.

Orange-throated Longclaw (*Macronyx capensis*). Here is a grassland bird that makes life a little easier for the bird-watcher, as after trying to identify dozens of frustratingly similar brown birds, the orange-throated longclaw will come as a pleasing surprise. When the bird is first seen, however, it will probably appear as just another dull brown back, but once the unmistakeable, vivid, orange sides to the throat are spotted, correct identification is assured. Males and females are similar, but the orange throats of juveniles are 'washed-out' compared with the brilliance of the adults. The very long hindclaws which characterize the species, considerably increase the spread of the feet and provide useful supports when walking over matted grass.

Pied Starling (*Spreo bicolor*). Most starlings on the African continent have a metallic sheen to their predominantly blue-green plumages and though the pied starling is brown, it too has a characteristic, but faint gloss to the upper wing feathers. The white vent is also distinctive. The species is gregarious and groups of a hundred or more birds may gather to forage on the ground, often near cattle or sheep. Like cattle egrets, pied starlings run and fly after insects disturbed by these animals as they browse through the veld. They may even perch on the backs of livestock and though the odd tick or grasshopper may be gleaned in this manner, these birds are more likely to be taking advantage of the added height to keep a look-out for food closer to the ground. Nests are built at the end of tunnels excavated deep into vertical banks, often where roads cut through hillsides. Several such nest holes may be packed into one small embankment.

Richard's Pipit (*Anthus novaeseelandiae*). The discarded barbel head holds little interest for this Richard's pipit as food, but it does provide a handy perch from which it watches for insects moving in the surrounding grass. Though

Richard's Pipit

the fish remains suggest habitats near water, this ubiquitous bird occurs throughout South Africa's grasslands. Pipits and larks are very similar, but pipits can be distinguished by their white outer tail feathers and more slender bodies. Stance is also characteristic as pipits stand with their legs straight, while larks tend to crouch. This is well illustrated by comparing the bird shown here with the rufous-naped lark. Differences between Richard's pipit and several other brown pipits are difficult to discern and the best way to identify this species is to learn its call and display. During the breeding season individuals frequently make high flights while uttering 'chiwrit' or 'priprit'. The display is ended with a steep dive to the ground.

Red-billed Quelea *(Quelea quelea)*. Hundreds of nests are crammed into a single bush, but this is a mere fraction of the whole breeding colony which may extend over many hectares. With each pair of red-billed queleas raising several young each season, it is easy to see why these grain-eating birds are regarded as Africa's 'number one' bird pest – a status that no other species even remotely approaches. In some areas, these queleas are known as 'locust birds', an apt description not only of their massive, dense flocks which seem to arrive out of nowhere, but also their ability to destroy fields of sorghum or millet within a few days. Aircraft are used to spray poison over their huge roosts and breeding colonies at night and the number of dead or stunned birds lying on the ground the following morning is quite staggering. Though farmers have the right to protect their livelihood, these control measures are anything but selective and it is unfortunate that many 'innocent' species also fall victim to such wholesale slaughters.

Orange-throated Longclaw

Pied Starling

Red-billed Quelea

Common Waxbill

Long-tailed Widow Bird *(Euplectes progne)*. The draping tail plumes of this proud male all but reach the ground as he perches atop a tall weed to cast a sharp eye about his domain. This showy dress is worn by adult males only during the breeding season and is very different from the brownish plumages of non-breeding males, females and juveniles. Breeding males are strongly territorial and once they have staked their claim to a specific area they set about advertising themselves to potential mates in 'dancing' flights low over the open grassland. During these very slow courtship flights the wings beat deeply and the long tail feathers curve gracefully downwards. Set against the uninterrupted veld, the striking black plumage and characteristic display make males clearly visible even at great distances. The long-tailed widow bird is polygamous and a single male frequently pairs with several females. Nest-building is a task left entirely to the females and each 'wife' occupies her own nest — a dense ball of woven grass well concealed in a tall stand of grass.

Common Waxbill *(Estrilda astrild)*. With its feathers fluffed for warmth against the winter chill, this lone bird shows clearly the characteristic thick red line along each side of the face. At close range, fine barring on the breast and belly may also be seen. The common waxbill is a lively little bird and is usually found in compact parties of a dozen or more individuals actively foraging for grass seed and small insects. Like all waxbills, the members of this species make untidy nests which resemble dense balls of fine grass. The entrance is always to the side. The rough workmanship has its purpose, however, as whether constructed in tufts of grass or in small bushes, the nest blends well with its surroundings. Four to seven eggs are laid, each of which measures only some 14 mm long and 11 mm wide. Should larger eggs be found in a common waxbill nest, these are likely to belong to the pin-tailed whydah which makes use of other species to incubate its eggs and raise its young. The common waxbill is a frequent 'choice' for this task. Unlike the parasitic cuckoo nestlings which eject the eggs or young of their hosts, the young of the pin-tailed whydah and the common waxbill may be reared in harmony.

Long-tailed Widow Bird

WETLANDS

In this chapter the term wetlands is used in the broadest sense to cover habitats ranging from small roadside puddles and water-logged ditches, to sewage farms, farm dams, and man-made reservoirs. The richest habitats, however, are natural marshes, lakes and flood plains. Unfortunately, large natural wetland areas in South Africa have been irrevocably destroyed by bulldozers and pumping schemes to make them suitable for industry and agriculture. Those disturbingly few that remain must be preserved as they provide a rich and vital food source and a protective breeding ground,

not only for the few species mentioned here, but also a host of others, both migrant and local.

Wetland regions worth visiting are the Milnerton and Rietvlei complex near Cape Town and the Strandfontein Ponds at Muizenberg. On the Reef, Marievale, Rondebult and Leeupan can provide rewarding hours of birding and the Nylsvlei flood plain near Nylstroom is surely the best birding marsh in South Africa. Natal has the St Lucia Lake region, the flood plains in the Mkuzi Reserve as well as those of the Pongola north to Ndumu. These areas are all superb waterbird habitats, but even a small farm dam surrounded by reeds can host many varied and interesting species.

African Darter (*Anhinga melanogaster*). The African darter earns its alternative name of 'snakebird' when ploughing through the water, body submerged and only the long skinny neck and head visible. An expert fisher, it lunges forward with a swift thrust of the head and neck, actually impaling prey on the dagger-sharp bill. The neck bones of the African darter are specially developed for this hunting technique. This close relative of the cormorant family is distinguished from similar species in South Africa by its long, thin, rufous neck and head, black and white striped back and very long tail. During the breeding season small colonies form, sometimes together with reed cormorants, herons and egrets. Nests are large, shapeless stick platforms and two or three eggs are laid. The newly-hatched young are covered in white snowy down.

Reed Cormorant (*Phalacrocorax africanus*). The smallest of the cormorants frequenting inland waters, the reed cormorant is distinguished from the African darter by its smaller size, short, hooked bill and tuft of upright feathers on the forehead during the breeding season. This gregarious bird nests in colonies, in reedbeds, or in trees where it makes a rough platform out of twigs and reeds. Despite being water dwellers, cormorants have coarse plumage which, unlike most swimming and diving birds, is not completely waterproof. Thus they frequently become waterlogged and spend many hours perched with wings and tail spread, drying their feathers. The wings are often spread in this manner even when the bird is dry, as the posture also serves to keep the bird warm and may be a signal to other reed cormorants.

White Pelican (*Pelecanus onocrotalus*). This is the pelican found commonly on the many vleis surrounding Cape Town and at Lake St Lucia in Zululand. It is identified by its large size, long capacious bill and white body with black flight feathers. The pelican is well known for the large distensible pouch hanging from the lower jaw and though it is commonly held that this is used for storing food, it is in fact a highly-specialized food gathering device which, when dipped below the surface, billows out like a net, scooping up fish and, sometimes, crustacea. White pelicans often fish in teams, many birds gliding along gracefully, shoulder to shoulder, scooping at the water in perfect synchrony when a shoal of small fish is encountered. Adult pelicans are heavy birds which weigh as much as 10–12 kilograms and this makes direct flight a somewhat laboured affair. To conserve energy on long flights, therefore, these birds ride rising hot air currents, or thermals, and often spiral to great heights before drifting off into the distance.

White-breasted Cormorant (*Phalacrocorax carbo*). A much larger bird than the reed cormorant, the adults of this species have shining white feathers on the throat, sides of the neck and breast. During the breeding season, males also have large white patches on the flanks which are very significant in courtship displays when the male bird takes an unusual stance on or near the nest, with the bill pointed upwards and the neck bent backwards. The partially closed wings are then flicked up and down to expose the white patches which gives the impression of flashing white lights, especially when seen against a dark background. This obvious display is thought to attract a mate. On very hot days white-breasted cormorants, like all members of the family, will resort to 'gular fluttering' or palpitating the throat — a technique for ridding the body of excess heat by rapidly drawing in and expelling air over the wet mouth and throat. This cormorant is the one 'harnessed' by the Chinese to catch fish.

African Darter

Reed Cormorant

White Pelican

White-breasted Cormorant

Grey-headed Gull

Grey-headed Gull *(Larus cirrocephalus)*. Gulls are usually thought of as seabirds, but though the grey-headed gull occurs in small numbers along the Natal coast, its preferred habitats are the marshlands of the hinterland, especially the fresh water lakes created by goldmining operations on the Reef and in the Free State. It rarely ventures as far south as the southern and western Cape coasts where it could be confused with the Hartlaub's gull, but even here the red legs and bill and silvery white eye would identify this gull. Furthermore the grey hood of the breeding plumage (shown here) is very distinctive. Large colonies nest on islands in marshes and lakes and adult birds protect these breeding territories with vigour, mobbing and dive-bombing and even sometimes striking an intruder. The young have mottled backs, a smudge of brown on the nape and show a black band on the tip of the tail.

Grey Heron *(Ardea cinerea)*. The yellow bill, black stripe above the eye ending in a wispy plume and the overall grey body identify this tall, almost gawky heron which can easily be overlooked when it stands motionless alongside reedbeds. In flight its long neck is drawn back and tucked into the body and its long broad wings beat slowly in powerful deeply-curved arcs. When fishing it stalks very slowly through the shallows on its long legs, suddenly stabbing the water with lightning speed to secure its prey. Although small fish and frogs are the major elements of the diet, the grey heron is also known to take the young of waterbirds such as ducks, moorhens and grebes. Breeding colonies occur in tall trees where bill-clappering, grunts and harsh 'kraark kraark' calls make up part of the courtship display.

Hamerkop *(Scopus umbretta)*. The long, slightly flattened bill and long chunky crest which in profile resemble the head of a hammer, make identification of this dark-brown bird relatively easy. In flight, however, when the crest is flattened along the back of the neck, the bird takes on an almost hawk-like appearance. The hamerkop is frequently seen along roadsides in the early morning feeding on frogs killed by traffic during the night, but though carrion can

Grey Heron

Goliath Heron

Hamerkop

Great White Egret

make up part of the diet, live prey such as frogs and other small aquatic animals are pursued along the banks of ponds and ditches. Huge, domed nests are built in trees and the entrance holes are difficult to get at as they are placed on the bottom or to the side.

Goliath Heron *(Ardea goliath).* As the name implies this is the largest of the herons, not only in South Africa, but also the world. It completely dwarfs all other members of the family and this feature alone serves to identify the bird. In flight, it is slow and ponderous, the long, broad wings being kept well arched in both the up and downward strokes. Take-off, too, is slow and awkward and at times the bird seems only to clear the ground by the merest of margins. It is generally very silent, but when disturbed or at the nest it calls a deep braying 'kwaak'. The goliath heron breeds either in colonies with other herons and egrets, or in isolated pairs and the nest is a bulky affair made from large sticks placed in the upper branches of a tree and usually contains three large pale blue eggs.

Great White Egret *(Egretta alba).* By far the largest egret in South Africa, this species is distinguished by its exceptionally long, slender neck and its bill which, though black for most of the year, is yellow during the September to March breeding season. The long, white, wispy tail plumes that are raised and fanned in courtship displays are also distinctive. The habitat of the great white egret varies considerably and the bird can be found from flooded meadows and farm dams to large lakes and marshes, all of which harbour a ready food supply of frogs and small fish. The long neck comes into its own during 'fishing' as the bird is able to thrust its head well below the surface. Unlike the cattle egret this species usually feeds alone, but does gather to form breeding colonies with other egrets and herons. Three or four large white eggs are laid and the nests are platforms of twigs and sticks constructed in trees overhanging water. At the turn of the century the great white egret was almost exterminated in Europe as its delicate white rump plumes were very fashionable in ladies' headwear.

Sacred Ibis

Spoonbill

Sacred Ibis *(Threskiornis aethiopicus).* This bird was held sacred by the Egyptians of dynastic times and it is depicted in many murals of that era, especially those in tombs. It is not understood, however, why the sacred ibis is no longer found in Egypt. Though the only white ibis in South Africa, the long downward-curving bill, naked black head and neck and blue-black scapular plumes of the sacred ibis rule out any possibility of confusion with other species. In flight, the white wings reveal black tips to the flight feathers, and, in the breeding season only, a naked strip of red skin is shown on the underwing. Breeding colonies are formed in reedbeds and trees in marshes and also the islands off the western Cape coast where nests are built among rocks or scrub vegetation. The sacred ibis is frequently found in the colonies of penguins, cormorants and gulls where it robs

Little Grebe

Yellow-billed Duck

Cape Teal

nests of eggs as well as young. The wanderings of these birds are not known to follow any migratory pattern, but they do, nevertheless, cover great distances in search of food and flocks are very often found foraging in open fields and ploughed lands far from water.

Spoonbill *(Platalea alba).* As the bird wades forward through the water it sweeps its spatular bill from side to side, sifting the bottom mud for the small aquatic life forms that make up its diet. The spoonbill is usually silent, but during courtship displays the long bill is opened and closed quickly, making a clapping sound. During the courting sequence, mutual preening and raising the head feathers while pointing the bill skyward, occur as well. Bill clappering is also part of an aggressive display towards other spoonbills impinging on its territory. If the intruder ignores this warning he is liable to incur the full wrath of the defending bird which may lunge forward, viciously pecking at the offender's head and body. Small parties of spoonbills occasionally join mixed heronries to breed, and place their nests in trees and sometimes in reedbeds. In flight the neck is held outstretched and this, combined with the long bill, gives the bird a very distinctive flight shape.

Little Grebe *(Tachybaptus ruficollis).* Also known as the dabchick, this little waterbird is found in the smallest ponds as well as the largest stretches of open water. It also undertakes nocturnal flights and flocks will suddenly appear overnight in freshly flooded areas. Though often very shy during the breeding season when it skulks amongst the reeds, at other times of the year it is quite commonly seen swimming and diving in pairs or small parties, calling a distinctive, whinnying trill. In summer breeding plumage the little grebe is easily recognized by its dark body, rufous throat and neck and white bottom. A small yellow spot at the base of the bill is also very noticeable. A peculiar habit is the exposing of a bare patch of black skin around the vent to the sun on cold days, especially in the early morning. In this manner solar energy is absorbed, helping to keep the bird warm.

Yellow-billed Duck *(Anas undulata).* Nondescript mottled brown plumage and chrome yellow sides to the bill identify this duck, and at close range a metallic blue-green patch is visible on the wings. The females make a strident 'quack quack' whilst the males have a higher-pitched, raspy call note. The nest is well concealed in thick vegetation on the ground near water and is lined with soft warm down plucked from the breast of the female. The generally drab plumage of the female serves as an excellent camouflage, but if discovered on the nest or with her brood, she commonly pretends injury and will frantically flap around in all directions, continually calling in simulated distress to draw attention from her ducklings while they make good their escape.

Cape Teal *(Anas capensis).* This small, perky duck with its slightly upturned, pinkish bill, greyish head and mottled greyish body, is easily identified. In flight the dark upperwings contrast with the body and show two white stripes. Though usually encountered in small parties or in pairs, in some areas of the western Cape these birds frequently form large flocks out of the breeding season. Nests are ground-level affairs, often under bushes and are lined with down which covers the eggs, keeping them warm when the nest is left untended for short periods. Cape teals often upend themselves in shallow water to scour the bottom for insects and vegetation, a habit which is typical of this and closely-related species. The Cape teal, however, also dives for food in deeper water, an unusual ability in surface-feeding ducks.

White-faced Whistling Duck *(Dendrocygna viduata)*. When alarmed this bird, like all whistling ducks, stands very erect on exceptionally long legs, the body almost vertical and the neck stretched to peer at the intruder. The white face patch which is often stained pinkish, the rusty brown breast and the heavily barred flanks are characteristic. Though the female African shelduck also has a white face, it differs by having a grey head and neck and large white forewing patches. The call is a shrill trisyllabic whistle, 'wee wee weeoe', which is rendered repeatedly while in flight. This whistling call is often heard at night when activity increases and probably helps flock members to keep in touch as they move from marshes to more open areas to feed.

Spurwing Goose *(Plectropterus gambensis)*. The spurwing is the largest goose in South Africa and is easily distinguished by its pied black and white plumage and pinkish legs and bill. The spurs of this and many other species are used as weapons of aggression and defence, but they are also believed by some biologists to be residual claws. Aeons back in time these claws helped birds to clamber through trees and to maintain balance. The fossil *Archaeopterix* had such claws and the hoatzin, a bird of today which lives in the jungles of Brazil, uses similar claws to help it cling to branches. Spurwing geese are frequently seen far from water striding around fields and grazing; they are particularly fond of lucerne and the considerable damage they can cause to these and other crops understandably puts them at odds with many farmers. Spurwings prefer to feed at night and they rest up during the day on large open areas of water, out of range of the hunter's gun. Nests are bulky and made from reeds, sparsely lined with feathers and down. The white eggs, 6–10 in number, are large and glossy.

Egyptian Goose *(Alopochen aegyptiacus)*. Despite the implication of its name, this bird is related more to the African shelduck than to the true goose family. In flight it closely resembles the shelduck, but has less white on the forewings and lacks the grey head of the male and white face of the female. Calls vary from the raspy hissing of the males to the conventional quacking and trumpeting of the females. When large flocks gather the Egyptian goose is very aggressive toward its fellow members. This behaviour is typical in flocking species where each individual, or pair, keeps to its own small territory. If this territory is intruded upon, the white forewings are displayed to intimidate the interloper and this is often a prelude to squabbling and fighting. The loser retreats and in this way the bigger and stronger birds

White-faced Whistling Duck

Spurwing Goose

Egyptian Goose

Red-billed Teal

Marsh Harrier

gain larger standing areas, usually at the centre of the flock where there is least danger from predators. The nests are often placed in trees and it is not uncommon for the old nest of a heron or even the top of a hamerkop's nest to be used.

Marsh Harrier *(Circus ranivorus).* The marsh harrier is shown here in its typical hunting flight, coursing low over reed beds and marshes only to disappear suddenly from view as it drops onto its prey which includes small birds, rodents and reptiles. The flight is buoyant and flapping while quartering the hunting territory, but when gliding the wings are held in a shallow 'V'. Though similar to the yellow-billed kite, the square-ended long tail of the marsh harrier as opposed to the forked tail of the kite, rules out confusion. The nest is placed on the ground in thick reedbeds or long grass and is a platform made of reeds and grasses. Three or four eggs are laid and are greenish white in colour.

Red-billed Teal *(Anas erythrorhyncha).* This duck is larger than the Cape teal and has a red, not pink, bill and is generally much darker in colour with a conspicuous dark brown cap. In flight it shows a buff patch on the secondaries. It is also more abundant and widespread in South Africa than the Cape teal and gathers in large flocks with other duck species. The female's call is a soft 'quack quack' while the male call is a thin buzzing hiss. Nests, lined with grass and down, are usually placed close to the water where they are concealed amongst reeds or thick grass.

Red-knobbed Coot (*Fulica cristata*). The all-black plumage of this waterbird is broken by the white bill and white 'shield' on the forehead. This species is distinguished by the two small red knobs on top of the white shield; however, these are inconspicuous and only noticeable during the breeding season when they become swollen as a signal to potential mates. The feet are not webbed but each toe has circular flattened lobes which increase the foot area and perform effectively as paddles. The coot is much more obvious and aggressive than the common moorhen which it resembles superficially, and swims and dives freely on open stretches. When disturbed it splatters across the surface with its lobed feet. Very often it will belly-flop back into the water without taking to the air, but if under serious threat it will continue flapping vigorously with its wings before gaining height. Once airborne, however, the red-knobbed coot flies strongly.

Common Moorhen (*Gallinula chloropus*). This small, black, hen-like bird has green legs, a yellow-tipped bill and white undertail which is constantly flicked when walking. Though lacking webbed feet, the moorhen often takes to the water, floating high and moving slowly forward, constantly jerking its head, neck and tail. It is rather shy, preferring to forage in sheltered reedbeds, and often the loud 'kurreeck' or 'kek kek' call is the only indication of its presence. Occasionally small flotillas will venture on to open water to feed, but will quickly dash for cover when disturbed. Diet consists of soft plants, seeds and insects taken whilst swimming or stalking around vegetation close to water. The nest is a platform of dried reeds placed over water in reedbeds, or in low bushes.

Treble-banded Sandplover (*Charadrius tricollaris*). The two black collars across the breast readily identify this plover and at close range the red base to the bill and red eye-ring are conspicuous. These birds are more often seen singly or

Red-knobbed Coot

Common Moorhen

African Jacana

in small groups and rarely congregate in large numbers like other plovers. Despite their common name, they prefer to feed along the margins of small muddy ponds or puddles rather than in sandy areas. Individuals are frequently heard before being spotted, and when located are usually standing still, but teetering curiously and bobbing both head and tail while calling 'chee eet chee eet'. The function of teetering and bobbing is not clearly understood, but may enable birds like the treble-banded sandplover, which have only side vision, to build up a three dimensional impression of an object by viewing it from different angles. The nest is a mere scrape amongst stones or on gravel, sometimes lined with small pebbles, and the two eggs blend well with their surroundings.

African Jacana (*Actophilornis africanus*). The ability to walk lightly over waterlily leaves and other floating vegetation has earned the 'lily trotter' its rather apt alias. This facility is made possible by the extra long toes and nails which distribute the jacana's mass over a large area rather in the manner of an Eskimo's snow-shoes. Small aquatic insects are favoured items of diet and are pecked from the surface as the bird flits from one piece of floating vegetation to another. The jacana walks upright with jerky movements and cocks its tail and occasionally, when alighting, raises its wings high over its back. Nests are made from rotting vegetation and are supported by waterlilies or thick matted floating weeds. The jacana provides a good example of the reversal of male and female roles. After laying the eggs which are chocolate-coloured and delicately patterned with fine black scribblings, the female moves on to take another mate and it becomes the sole responsibility of the male to incubate the eggs and to tend the chicks until they can fly. This behaviour is unusual amongst birds and is only possible in environments like that of the jacana where food is abundant.

Treble-banded Sandplover

White-winged Black Tern

Wood Sandpiper (*Tringa glareola*). A migrant from the northern hemisphere, the wood sandpiper arrives in South Africa in September and stays only for the summer months. It is very shy and unobtrusive and more often than not it is only seen when flushed from cover as it dashes off speedily, showing its small white rump and calling a shrill 'chiff if if'. On the ground, or wading through shallow water, it darts around quickly snapping up insects and other small aquatic creatures. Like the treble-banded sandplover, this species teeters while standing and also occasionally flicks its wings over its back when alighting.

White-winged Black Tern (*Chlidonias leucopterus*). A lone tern 'rides' the air, but huge flocks are more common near freshwater ponds in the southern Cape. Such behaviour is typical during March and April when, with autumn drawing in, flocks of over a thousand birds may gather before migrat-

ing north. Breeding takes place in Europe and Asia during summer and birdwatchers in South Africa are seldom treated to the display plumage which shows a striking contrast between silvery upper wings and smokey-black body and head. In its drab, non-breeding dress the white-winged black tern is easily confused with the black tern and is only distinguished by its generally paler plumage and the lack of small dark shoulder smudges. Unlike most other terns this species does not plunge into water to catch food, but gracefully and with seeming weightlessness flits low over the surface dipping its beak now and then to secure some small aquatic animal.

Red Bishop (*Euplectes orix*). The male (shown here) combines brilliant scarlet and black in a striking plumage that is held only for the few months of breeding – for the rest of the year he resembles the female with sparrow-like, dowdy,

Wood Sandpiper

Red Bishop

Cape Weaver

brown-speckled plumage. During this short colourful season males frequently perform attention-getting flights over their colonies, puffing out their black bellies and rump feathers and whirring around in all directions like huge bumble bees. Each male makes several neatly-woven, dome-shaped nests which are attached to reed stalks and then sets about enticing female takers by his frenetic flights and by puffing up his feathers and calling an excited 'chik chik chik chik'. The more successful males sometimes have two or three 'wives' at one time.

Cape Weaver *(Ploceus capensis)*. The male, here, shows off his bright breeding plumage, the creamy coloured eyes alert to both danger and suitable nesting sites. Males in non-breeding plumage, however, resemble the females who are dull olive green above and buffy yellow below. Their nesting colonies, situated either in reed beds or hanging from trees

growing over water, are noisy and constantly bustle with activity. Individual nests are beautifully woven by the males from grasses and strips of reed. The males then hang from the downward facing entrances to their newly-completed nests and proclaim their prowess by swaying to and fro flapping their wings and uttering swizzling calls in the hope of attracting a mate while also declaring their dominance over their territory. Weaving is not a skill taught to the young Cape weavers by their parents, but is largely an inherited facility. This has been shown by hatching and rearing young weavers in captivity without them ever seeing their parents or any other bird. When the males in this study reached maturity they were supplied with materials for weaving nests and though their first few attempts were poor, eventually they were able to construct nests comparable to those of their parents.

Levaillant's Cisticola

Levaillant's Cisticola *(Cisticola tinniens)*. The cisticolas are a group of warblers notoriously difficult to identify, this species being no exception. In the southern and eastern Cape it is usually the common cisticola that is found in reed beds and long grass surrounding marshes and ponds, but in wetlands elsewhere in South Africa it can be confused with similar species. Its 'chee chee chirrupee' call, however, is distinctive and a certain identification. As shown here, it is not a shy bird and will flit onto grass or reed stems to peer at, or scold any intruder. The nest is placed well down at the base of reeds or grass and is made from fine grass which is lined with the soft down or 'hair' of windborne seeds.

Pied Kingfisher *(Ceryle rudis)*. This unmistakable black and white bird is frequently seen over water, bill pointing downwards, tail depressed and sharp eyes scanning the surface as it hovers, ready to plummet headfirst in pursuit of a meal. Males have two black breast bands and the female (shown here) has one. The call is a loud screeching cackle uttered either in flight or when at rest on some exposed perch while flicking its short tail up and down. The nest is placed at the end of a long tunnel excavated into a bank and is characterised by a strong and unpleasant fishy odour emanating from the entrance. This comes from the regurgitated fish bones which the kingfishers and their young are unable to digest, as well as from the excrement of the nestlings which are not, as with some burrowing birds, deposited in faecal sacs and removed from the nest by the parents.

Malachite Kingfisher *(Alcedo cristata)*. Streaking low over the water it appears much like a jewelled dart and even here, poised quietly on the end of a broken branch the colours of the malachite kingfisher are spectacular. Perched on a low branch or reed overlooking water, it regularly bobs its head or watches the surface intently for prey, plunging into the water as a suitable meal comes within range. If successful, the fish is carried to a branch or rock and the bird proceeds to bash it from side to side, presumably to kill it before swallowing. The kingfisher then juggles the fish in its bill to ensure that the head is swallowed first, to prevent the fins and gills from opening and lodging in the bird's throat—with fatal results.

Pied Kingfisher

Malachite Kingfisher

BUSHVELD

Where South Africa's high central plateau dips to the east and north, the grassland plains give way to the tree-dominated landscape of the bushveld — a broad tract of land that sweeps in a great arc from north-eastern Zululand, through Swaziland, the eastern and northern parts of the Transvaal, into Zimbabwe and beyond. In the drier areas, acacias and the baobab prevail, but where the rains are heavier, broad-leafed trees such as the mopane, *Combretum* and *Terminalia* may form an almost-continuous woodland canopy.

Some bushveld birds are large and obvious, but many are small insectivores that creep through the trees gleaning prey from the foliage or pecking it from the bark. These birds frequently form parties that may comprise ten or more species. As parties move systematically through the trees in search of food, so there is a continuous coming and going as some birds drop out and others join in. When a tree is found with a particularly rich insect population, the birds gather together and will often remain until the food supply is exhausted before moving on.

It is always fruitful to find a bird party and follow it, for within a very short time the birdwatcher will be rewarded

Marabou Stork

with good views of several species. Another easy way to observe bushveld birds is to find a quiet, reasonably concealed position and call repeatedly 'spsh . . . spsh', or 'pish . . . pish . . . pish'. A wide variety of species is likely to respond and some will venture close.

The best birding areas in the bushveld are undoubtedly the protected reserves in the eastern Transvaal and northern Natal. The Kruger National Park and Mkuze Game Reserve, in particular, will each provide at least 200 species which can be easily seen.

Marabou Stork *(Leptoptilos crumeniferus).* The marabou stork stands over a metre tall on its long, spindly legs and has a wingspan of more than three times its height. Its size, ugly bald red head and neck, throat pouch and massive bill make this forbidding bushveld scavenger unmistakable. The group shown here is combing the veld for insects and lizards, but the marabou stork is also commonly seen marching around animal carcasses snatching up scraps of flesh. Scavengers generally consume large quantities of food as they often have to survive for long periods between meals. Not surprisingly, this predilection for carrion frequently leads to marabous and vultures feeding off the same carcass. Direct competition is avoided, however, as marabous concentrate on small scraps that tend to be ignored by vultures. In common with a number of other storks, the marabou often has white-coloured legs. The whiteness is, in fact, a layer of uric acid that comes from defaecating down the legs. This seeming incontinence has a function as in hot weather the liquid excreta cools the legs and thus helps to rid the body of excess heat.

White-backed Vulture *(Gyps africanus).* The unattractive bald head and neck of birds that are specialist scavengers is appropriate to their equally unattractive, but necessary, habit of delving deep within a carcass; feathers on these difficult-to-reach parts of the body would soon become clogged with decaying flesh and dry blood. This species is the most common of the bushveld vultures, particularly in the eastern Transvaal and Zululand game reserves. The white back is only visible when the wings are spread, but,

Yellow-billed Kite

taken with the dark eyes, serves to distinguish the species from the very similar, pale-eyed, Cape vulture. Juveniles, like the bird in the bottom left hand corner, are dark brown overall. This vulture nests in large trees, often along rivers, and several pairs may nest close to one another, giving the appearance of a loose colony. Non-breeding birds roost communally. In the morning they may remain at their roosts for several hours until the day has warmed sufficiently to produce thermals. These rising columns of air help lift them high into their holding positions from where they survey the ground for any sign of a meal.

Yellow-billed Kite *(Milvus migrans).* This kite is a summer visitor to South Africa; it arrives in August and September and returns northwards in March and April. During its stay, the yellow-billed kite occurs throughout the country, but is especially common in the bushveld. This large brown bird

Tawny Eagle

White-backed Vulture

of prey is usually seen gliding 10-30 metres above the ground, frequently following roads in search of small animals killed by motor traffic. Though some live prey is taken, this is usually confined to rodents, lizards and small birds as well as a number of insects. Its flight is relaxed and the wings are seldom flapped. The large tail acts as a rudder and is continually flexed from side to side to make directional adjustments. The distinctive flight silhouette, particularly the slightly forked, fan-shaped tail, makes identification easy. Specimens with yellow bills are breeding migrants to South Africa, while those with dark bills are immature birds or non-breeding adults which have nested in Europe and Asia.

Tawny Eagle *(Aquila rapax)*. This species is superficially very similar to Wahlberg's eagle. Both are basically 'brown eagles', but the tawny eagle is larger and has a relatively shorter tail and broader wings. It is most common in the eastern Transvaal and the northern Cape. Though not a gregarious bird, it will occasionally congregate in flocks around termite nests and red-billed quelea colonies, undoubtedly attracted by the overwhelming abundance and accessibility of food. The diet also includes small animals and game birds, but, like many birds of prey, the tawny eagle is not averse to carrion and is quite often among the first arrivals at a fresh kill. As shown here, the nest is a large structure placed in the canopy of a tall tree. Two eggs are laid in winter and though both hatch, only one nestling is usually raised. This is a common occurrence with raptors and is the result of a 'winner-takes-all' rivalry between the newly-hatched young. The young tawny eagle is fledged in spring when its plumage is still very pale, but with successive moults it becomes darker until adulthood is reached some four years later.

Wahlberg's Eagle

Lizard Buzzard

Cape Turtle Dove

Wahlberg's Eagle *(Aquila wahlbergi).* Most eagle species in South Africa are resident, with individuals or family groups occupying set territories throughout the year. Wahlberg's eagle is an exception, however, as it visits the region for the summer months only and migrates to equatorial Africa with the onset of colder weather. The precise location of its winter quarters is unknown. Plumage is uniformly brown and while most Wahlberg's eagles are dark, there are also many pale individuals. This variation is not related to age or sex. In flight, the rather long, narrow, square-edged tail is very distinctive as most other eagles have pronounced, fan-shaped tails. At close range, the birdwatcher may also notice the small crest which is a diagnostic feature of the species and the feathered legs which characterize all true eagles.

Lizard Buzzard *(Kaupifalco monogrammicus).* Many birds of prey are difficult to identify because of the marked plumage variations between the members of a single species. Adults, for example, frequently differ from young birds and adults may themselves display diverse plumages. To add to the confusion, these differences also often occur, as in the case of Wahlberg's eagle, irrespective of age or sex. The lizard buzzard, however, does not present this problem as the same plumage is worn by birds of both sexes and all ages. The most distinctive features of this overall grey raptor are the vertical black line on the throat and the large white rump. The red legs are also characteristic. Its flight is direct and though it does occasionally soar, the lizard buzzard is more commonly seen flying low and hard, displaying its conspicuous white rump as it rises up into a tree. When hunting, this buzzard adopts a 'wait-and-see' strategy and perches quietly in a tree while it scans the ground for any lizard or mouse that ventures into the open.

Crested Francolin *(Francolinus sephaena).* The crested francolin is common in the Transvaal lowveld as well as other humid bushveld areas. It is most readily distinguished from other, very similar, francolins by its rather long and often slightly cocked tail, dark cap and freckled breast. It is an inconspicuous bird which spends a great deal of time skulking through the undergrowth and is usually only seen, very briefly, in small family parties crossing a bushveld road. The call, however, is a most distinctive and frequently repeated, 'wary . wetchi . . . wary . wetchi'. The nest is a shallow bowl, lined with grass and well concealed in thick cover. It usually holds between five and eight off-white eggs which hatch within three weeks of being laid. The young are soon able to follow their parents and by the time they are half-grown they can manage short flights.

Cape Turtle Dove *(Streptopelia capicola).* The common name of this bird suggests a somewhat limited distribution. Nothing could be more misleading as the Cape turtle dove is one of the most common and numerous birds throughout southern Africa. It is, however, most abundant in the bushveld, particularly the drier areas, where its repetitive 'coo . koorr . . coo . koorr' calls are among the most familiar sounds. The distinctive features of this species are the black collar and the pattern of white on the tail. It does not have red around the eye and this reduces the possibility of confusion with the similar, red-eyed turtle dove. The male Cape turtle dove conducts regular displays when it climbs high above the trees in a vigorous flapping flight and then glides back to its perch. These performances, typical of many doves which occupy set territories, probably serve to advertise the bird's position to possible competitors. While nest building is the task of the female Cape turtle dove, the male collects the construction material. The nest is flimsy and is seldom used for breeding more than once.

Crested Francolin

Meyer's Parrot *(Poicephalus meyeri).* Compared with Australia or South America, Africa has few parrots and these are also less colourful than their overseas relatives. Meyer's parrot is quite common in some bushveld areas, where it is usually seen in small parties of six or so birds. More may congregate in fruiting trees. Unfortunately, this alert and wary species seldom allows anyone to approach closely and the best way to obtain good views is to wait quietly beneath a fig tree in fruit. Meyer's parrot is very noisy in flight and its harsh screams draw immediate attention as it flies rapidly and deftly through the woodland canopy. The great multipurpose beak is equally suited to carving soft fruit, cracking seed or grasping branches as the bird clambers through the foliage. The nest is placed in a tree hole and two or three white eggs are laid.

Emerald-spotted Wood Dove *(Turtur chalcospilos).* Poised at this muddy pool-edge, an emerald-spotted wood dove prepares to drink, the glossy-green wing spots conspicuous in the slanting sunlight. In duller light these patches are less obvious and appear very dark. This small dove, however, is more often heard than seen. Its monotonous call carries far and permeates most humid woodland areas. It consists of a series of 'du' sounds, the first few notes being repeated slowly. The final run of about ten 'du's are delivered at increasing speed, but become softer until finally fading away. The emerald-spotted wood dove is swift and adept at rapid changes of direction as it weaves its way through the woodland. In flight, the wings appear russet while the rump shows two horizontal black bands.

Diederik Cuckoo *(Chrysococcyx caprius).* The common name of the species is derived from its characteristic 'dee .. dee . diederik' call. Males are bright glossy-green above and largely white below with a few green bars on the flanks. Females are similar, but are more spotted below and more

Meyer's Parrot

bronzy above. Most cuckoos are parasitic breeders and make use of other birds to incubate their eggs and raise their young. This species is no exception, and here a masked weaver foster parent (left) feeds its much larger 'offspring', a fledgling diederik cuckoo. Weavers and sparrows are frequent hosts to the cuckoo young and in the early breeding season it is common to see these small birds frantically chasing cuckoos away from their nests. The male cuckoo is more boisterous than his mate and is, therefore, pursued with greater vigour. This routine is probably part of the cuckoo's breeding strategy; by enticing the prospective hosts away from the nest in this manner, the quieter female cuckoo is given the few moments she needs to slip unnoticed into the sparrow or weaver nest and lay her egg.

Grey Loerie (*Corythaixoides concolor*). This is the notorious 'go-away bird' that is reputedly the bane of the hunter's life, for at the first glimpse of a predator, the grey loerie launches into its distinctive 'quear . . . quear . . .' call. Repeated continuously, this abrasive signal probably alerts nearby animals to the approaching danger and often the hunter is obliged to 'go away' and try again. The grey loerie feeds largely on berries picked as it hops and clambers nimbly through leafy fruit trees. In flight, however, the bird is less agile and with rapidly-flapping wings and its long tail trailing behind, it labours from tree to tree. Nests are flimsy twig platforms and two or three pale blue eggs are laid. The development of the young differs from that of most tree-nesting birds as juvenile grey loeries leave the nest when they are only half-grown. They are unable to fly, however, and are confined to the nest tree until they fledge, some five to six weeks after hatching. All grey loeries, irrespective of age and sex, have a small crest and a completely grey plumage. Despite its many characteristics, these features alone would distinguish it from all other birds in South Africa.

Emerald-spotted Wood Dove

Diederik Cuckoo (juvenile (right))

Grey Loerie

Pearl-spotted Owl

Pearl-spotted Owl *(Glaucidium perlatum)*. At night, drongos, bulbuls and white-eyes may be regularly victimized by owls, but come daytime 'revenge' is exacted in return, as any owl found resting deep within a tree is unmercifully mobbed by these and other small birds. The pearl-spotted owl does not escape such harassment even though being small it hardly resembles the majority of owls. In fact this species is probably mobbed more than most as it makes little effort to conceal itself and is also, atypically for owls, quite often active by day. During its diurnal sorties, the pearl-spotted owl can be seen flying between trees, calling repeatedly, and occassionally even taking prey. The call comprises a series of ascending whistles followed by further, slurred whistles which sound precisely like the second note of a 'wolf whistle'. Birders can often attract several 'mobbing' species by imitating this distinctive call.

Giant Eagle Owl *(Bubo lacteus)*. This large owl stands about 600 mm tall and has a wingspan more than twice its height. At night its presence is indicated by muffled 'huhu . . . huhu' hoots. Despite superb night vision, this and other owl species rely more on ultra-sensitive hearing in the location of prey and even the slightest squeak or scuffle does not escape notice. The ears are located asymmetrically on either side of the head and by turning the head from side to side, the position of a prospective meal is soon 'fixed'. In the silent downward swoop that ensues, the eyes assist, probing even the deepest shadow as these birds home in on their prey. The giant eagle owl shown here has just returned from a successful hunt with a meal for its young, the amorphous bundle of feathers clinging to the near side of the nest. This species does not build its own nest, and while the eyrie of a

Giant Eagle Owl

large eagle is frequently usurped, hollow trees and the tops of social weaver or hamerkop nests are also used. The pink eyelids are diagnostic as is the overall pale plumage which affords good camouflage during the day when the bird huddles close to the trunk of a tall tree.

Woodland Kingfisher *(Halcyon senegalensis).* Like a number of kingfishers this species lives independently of water. It does not catch fish and does not even drink, as its diet of insects and, occasionally, small reptiles holds sufficient moisture for its needs. Though distributed throughout the bushveld, this kingfisher is most abundant in areas of moist broadleaf woodland where it frequently perches in trees overlooking clearings. From such high look-outs the woodland kingfisher scans the ground, poised to swoop down on prey that ventures into the open. The vivid blue area on the wings is a feature shared by several members of the family, but the red and black bill of this species helps to prevent confusion. The loud, ringing call, reminiscent of an alarm clock's jarring note, is also characteristic. This abrasive sound is repeated frequently, especially during the breeding season. While calling, the wings are also opened and closed to flash the blue and black flight-feathers.

European Bee-eater *(Merops apiaster).* Each spring, thousands of these colourful little birds arrive in South Africa from their breeding quarters in Europe. In addition, there is also a small population of nesting birds in the Cape, but little is known of their movements. The yellow throat, blue chest and belly, and the golden-brown back, aid identification and the plaintive, liquid 'kurr', often heard as they fly high overhead, is also most distinctive. As with other bee-eaters, the members of this species are entirely insectivorous and much of their prey is taken on the wing. Despite the common name, these birds do not specialize in catching bees, but should one of these insects be taken, the long bill provides a useful tool for safe, long-distance manipulation.

White-fronted Bee-eater *(Merops bullockoides).* The white chin and forehead combined with the bright red patch on the throat, make identification of this species relatively easy as no other bee-eater in South Africa has these markings. During the breeding season colonies form and a vertical bank is usually chosen as the nesting site. Here the birds drive tunnels as deep as half a metre into the soft soil. Each tunnel opens into a round nest chamber which normally holds a clutch of four white eggs. Individual nests are probably attended by a single pair and several subordinates. These 'helpers' are younger birds, usually the offspring of a previous mating, which assist the parents by keeping the nestlings well-provided with insects. Even in the non-breeding season this species usually associates in small groups, and at night, large numbers may roost communally in trees.

Lilac-breasted roller *(Coracias caudata).* All rollers are very colourful and conspicuous, especially during the twisting, tumbling courtship flights that give them their common name. The lilac-breasted roller is often tame and frequently perches prominently. This habit, combined with the pale chest, long tail streamers and vivid blue flight feathers, understandably makes this bird a favourite with many wildlife photographers. Adult lilac-breasted rollers stand about 150 mm tall and though the diet consists mostly of insects, these birds are large enough to prey on small lizards and mice when these are available. In common with many insect-eaters these rollers are attracted by veld fires and will patrol the edges of blazes while gleaning the insects driven before the advancing flames. Lilac-breasted rollers nest in tree holes, but do not excavate their own cavities.

European Bee-eater

Woodland Kingfisher

Lilac-breasted roller

White-fronted Bee-eater

Red-billed Hornbill

Red-billed Hoopoe *(Phoeniculus purpureus)*. Hoopoes are closely related to hornbills and this species shares the habit of the ground hornbill of living in groups, the members of which remain together throughout the year. Strong bonds develop within the group which co-operates not only in maintaining the territory, but also with the feeding of nesting females and their young. The female nests in a tree hole, often one vacated by a barbet or woodpecker and here, while she incubates the eggs, her mate, previous offspring and other members of the group all bring food to her and later her nestlings. Adult red-billed hoopoes are distinguished by their red, curved bills and beautiful metallic plumage. The young are similar, but have black bills. The call is a distinctive cackle, likened by the Zulu to a group of laughing women. When taken up by the group as a whole, this raucous clamour probably serves to advertise its presence – and its territorial claim – to other groups of the same species.

Red-billed Hornbill *(Tockus erythrorhynchus)*. About 400 mm long and 150 mm tall, these long, low-slung birds are a common sight at picnic spots in the Kruger National Park, where they bound about on short legs, always ready to grab morsels of food left lying around. The red bill is distinctive in males and females of all ages. In flight, a row of white dots on each of the flight feathers should prevent confusion with other hornbill species. Hornbills have a remarkable breeding strategy. Using a mixture of mud, debris and saliva, the female cements herself into her tree hole, but leaves open a narrow slit through which the male feeds her. Warmly closeted within the cavity, she sheds her tail and wing feathers while incubating the eggs. When the chicks are half-grown, the female, with her plumage renewed, breaks out of the nest. The cavity is immediately re-sealed by the young which remain within the nest, while the female joins her partner in feeding their brood. Up until this point, responsibility for successful breeding rests entirely with the male.

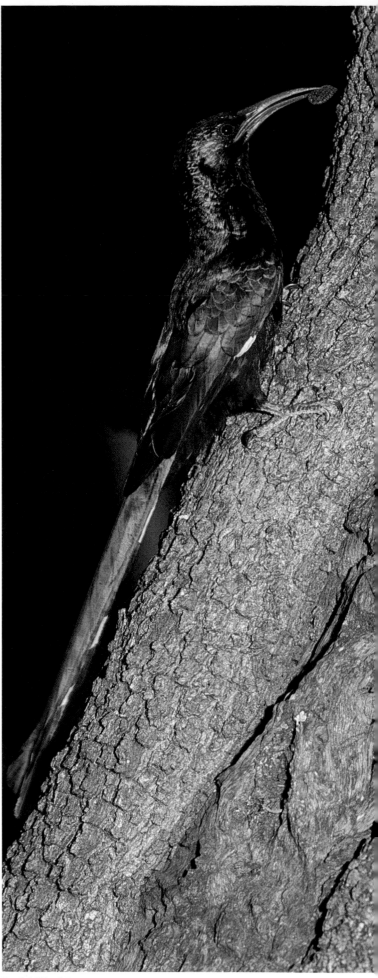

Red-billed Hoopoe

Ground Hornbill

Crested Barbet

Ground Hornbill *(Bucorvus leadbeateri)*. These hefty, turkey-sized birds – sometimes called turkey bustards – are powerful predators. Not only do they feed on insects, small reptiles and frogs, but are equally capable of dispatching game birds, large snakes and tortoises. The great bill is also often used to dig up frogs buried up to 300 mm beneath the surface. In this easily-recognized species, the scarlet pouch, beneath the bill, indicates adulthood; younger birds have yellowish-grey pouches. This huge pouch is usually distended and probably provides a suitable surface for losing excess heat. Normally seen in groups of three to seven individuals, ground hornbills spend much of the day waddling ponderously through the veld in search of a meal. They are, however, not entirely earth-bound and will take to the wing, revealing striking white primary wing feathers. In the course of their daily search for food, ground hornbills cover great distances and, by co-operating as a group in feeding the young, the amount of travel by each individual is greatly reduced. These birds nest in large tree holes usually containing a single nestling.

Crested Barbet *(Trachyphonus vaillantii)*. This barbet is unlikely to be confused with any other, as the crest, predominantly yellow underparts and speckled plumage are conspicuous. The call of the crested barbet is also characteristic, not unlike a fairly persistent alarm clock and may last unabated for up to 20 seconds. The nest hole is excavated in a tree and the eggs are laid on a bed of wood chips several centimetres below the entrance. A wide range of food is eaten, though insects – particularly termites – and berries are favoured. It is the only barbet in South Africa to feed occasionally on the ground. While essentially a bushveld bird living in wooded regions along rivers and water courses, today, with the planting of trees in the urban areas of Johannesburg and Pretoria, the crested barbet has extended its range and is common in these cities.

Sabota Lark

Sabota Lark *(Mirafra sabota)*. Most larks live in reasonably open grassland, but the sabota lark is a common bushveld bird. It regularly perches in trees, particularly after being disturbed while feeding on the ground. The large, white eye-stripe, rather short, thick bill and small size – adults are only about 80 mm tall – are useful identification features. In the breeding season, males sing from tree perches, but their song is quiet and unobtrusive. This lark builds its nest on the ground where it is often hidden beneath tufts of grass or small shrubs. Two or three white, speckled eggs are laid during the summer months.

Fork-tailed Drongo *(Dicrurus adsimilis)*. Impudent and fearless, the fork-tailed drongo is always game to take on predators as large as cats and snakes and will even swoop at huge raptors. The loud mobbing call is quite variable, sometimes a rasping twang and often with a metallic quality. Fork-tailed drongos are usually seen in pairs, perching prominently on exposed branches and darting after flying insects. They also freely take insects on the ground, and often follow lawn-mowers to catch those flushed from cover. The bird shown here is immature and still wears white-flecked breast feathers. Adults are uniformly glossy black, and the forked tail is obvious in birds of all ages.

Arrow-marked Babbler *(Turdoides jardineii)*. Loud, raucous cackling draws attention to the arrow-marked babblers' presence long before they are sighted. These insectivorous birds forage among bushes and among leaf litter for their prey. They live in groups of six to eight individuals which apparently remain together for most of the year. Each group defends a territory, a strategy common to many babbler species. Only the dominant female lays eggs and the rest of the group feeds both her and the nestlings. This behaviour extends to a predator-alarm system as well. At the approach of potential danger, the birds are quick to give a warning by all calling simultaneously, resulting in a deafening racket. The arrow-marks on the breast are distinctive, but only conspicuous at close range.

Groundscraper Thrush *(Turdus litsitsirupa)*. As its common name suggests, this species spends much of its time on the ground, quickly running a few metres, suddenly stopping, and then diving into leaf litter to scratch for insects. It is most common in moist woodland areas. Key features in identification include the heavily-spotted underparts, the two black lines on the sides of the face and the greyish back. The young by and large resemble their parents. In flight, all show orange-brown 'windows' on the wings. Thrushes are fine songsters, but performances are mainly reserved for the breeding season. This species calls while perched in leafy trees, and the scientific name, if rendered 'lit..sit.sirupa', is reminiscent of its whistle.

White-browed Scrub Robin *(Erythropygia leucophrys)*. Early in the bushveld morning or at dusk a series of very clear whistles, repeated over and over, is likely to be heard. This is the intriguing song of the scrub robin. It is difficult, however, to pin-point the source, for this bird is usually secretive and skulks well within the tangled shrubs. By calling 'spsh . . . spsh', as described in the introduction to this chapter, the birder may succeed in drawing this robin into the open. As the photograph clearly shows, the scrub robin builds its cup-shaped nest low in vegetation and here lays two or three freckled eggs.

Fork-tailed Drongo

Arrow-marked Babbler

Groundscraper Thrush

White-browed Scrub Robin

65

Neddicky *(Cisticola fulvicapilla).* The neddicky is one of the most nondescript birds of the bushveld, but once recognized, is a familiar sight in many places. A russet-brown cap, medium-length tail and unmarked back – other cisticolas usually have streaked ones – aid identification. Neddickys may become very tame and will hop within a few metres of an observer. They respond quickly to the birder's 'spsh . . . spsh' call described in the introduction to this chapter. Their diet consists of small insects gleaned as the birds hop through bushes and scratch around on the ground. Each nest is a ball of woven grass placed in a tuft of grass, usually close to a bush. The eggs vary greatly in colour and between three and five are normally laid.

Crombec *(Sylvietta rufescens).* The most noticeable feature of this tiny, otherwise undistinguished bird is its very short tail which sometimes seems almost absent. This, together with the uniform grey back and orange-brown underparts, confirms identification. In short, undulating flights, the crombec moves from tree to tree where much time is spent gleaning insects from leaves, or, as the bird shown here is doing, seeking insects hidden in the bark. It will often join foraging parties comprising several species of small insectivorous birds. By grouping together in this way, individuals probably find trees with good food supplies more easily than if they had searched alone. The crombec nest, suspended from a branch, is essentially purse-shaped, with one side extended and attached to the supporting branch.

Rattling Cisticola *(Cisticola chiniana).* This very common bushveld resident stands about 80 mm tall and its overall brownish plumage, lacking distinctive features, makes visual identification difficult. The call, however, is most characteristic. During the breeding season males perch in tree-tops

Crombec

Rattling Cisticola

Neddicky

Chin-spot Batis

and call 'chee . . . chee . . . chee . . . churrr'. This theme of two or three whistling notes, followed by a long rattle, does not vary. At close range, the mouth opened in song reveals the breeding male's black palate, an obvious feature, but common to several species. When alarmed, the rattling cisticola gives forth an admonishing and harsh 'shair . . . shair . . .'. It is quite bold and quick to scold potential predators and intruders near the nest.

Chin-spot Batis (Batis molitor). This boldly-coloured little batis is often seen in parties with other insectivorous birds moving quietly through the woodland canopy. Males and females differ in plumage. The common name derives from the females' brown breast-band and well-defined rufous chin-spot. As the photograph shows, however, males lack the chin-spot and have a black breast-band. The nest of this bird has a whimsical quality for it is camouflaged by deli-

cate flakes of lichen lifted from nearby branches and fixed with cobwebs. The nest in the photograph shows how effectively this structure melds with its surroundings. Two or three eggs are laid and the chicks soon crowd the small nest.

Crimson-breasted Shrike (Laniarius atrococcineus). As one of the most boldly marked birds in South Africa, this handsome species adds a dash of brilliant colour to the often drab bushveld. It is most common in the dry western Transvaal bush, but is also often seen in thornveld patches around Pretoria and Johannesburg. As with all shrikes, this species feeds mainly on insects, but unlike the blatant posturing of the fiscal shrike, the crimson-breasted shrike spends much of its time skulking through tangled thickets. The call, a loud, and frequently-rendered, whistling duet between the male and female, probably helps the pair maintain contact in thick cover where visibility is restricted.

Crimson-breasted Shrike

Three-streaked Tchagra

Three-streaked Tchagra *(Tchagra australis)*. Tchagras are members of the shrike family and spend much of their time skulking in thick cover. The three-streaked tchagra is best identified by its russet flight-feathers, pale beige under-parts, brown cap and strong black stripes on either side of the white band just above the eye. Males and females have similar plumage, but young birds are slightly duller. In the breeding season, displaying males leave the protection of the thick undergrowth to fly straight up above the woodland canopy and then to flutter down calling 'twuri . twuri . twuri . . .'. This species is entirely insectivorous, foraging among foliage as well as the leaf litter below bushes. The nest is cup-shaped, often placed low down in shrubs and usually holds two or three white eggs overlaid with bold, dark grey and brown marks.

Red-backed Shrike *(Lanius collurio)*. This shrike is a very common summer migrant from Europe and Asia. Like most other such migrants, it comes here as a non-breeding visitor. Red-backed shrikes spend much of their time perched on vantage-points overlooking small clearings in the bush. They seldom perch more than two metres off the ground and from here they dart out to grab passing insects. With the fiscal shrike, this species shares, on occasion, the seemingly grisly habit of impaling its prey on thorns. The male, pictured here, shows the characteristic russet back and black line through the eye. Females and young birds are alike, but with their drab, brown backs and fine barring on the breast and belly, are more reminiscent of flycatchers than shrikes.

White Helmet Shrike *(Prionops plumata)*. Helmet shrikes are always seen in small parties of up to a dozen or so birds. The flock remains together for long periods and though during the breeding season pairs may build their own nests, members co-operate with incubating the eggs and tending the young. Feeding parties are usually seen low down in small trees, creeping through the foliage in search of insects.

Red-backed Shrike

White Helmet Shrike

68

Cape Glossy Starling

The grey and white plumage is distinctive and, in flight, the birds show a flashing wing pattern in dark grey and white. Stiff bristly feathers on the forehead give the bird its common as well as its scientific name. In some areas of Africa the yellow eye-ring, clearly shown here, may be very large and conspicuous. The gossamer-shrouded nest is a finely-woven structure, neatly fastened with cobwebs to a branch.

Cape Glossy Starling *(Lamprotornis nitens)*. These dazzling birds are very common, especially scrounging around picnic spots in the southern Kruger National Park. More usually they scratch for insects and berries and are frequently seen in areas where cattle and other large mammals congregate. Here they glean insects flushed from the grass by the browsing animals. The species is normally encountered in small flocks, but close associations between individuals are not apparent. Nests are built in natural cavities such as tree holes and, in more recent times, hollow metal fence posts. Each one is lined with grass and three or four greenish-blue eggs are laid, usually during the summer months.

Marico Sunbird *(Nectarinia mariquensis)*. The resplendent male Marico sunbird will catch the eye of most observers in the bushveld. The metallic dorsal and breast feathering often catches the sunlight in a kaleidoscopic display. The purplish breast-band and black belly are diagnostic as these contrast with the bright red band and paler belly of certain other sunbirds. Females and young birds, however, are drab and difficult to identify with their dull, pale, but darkly-streaked brown fronts and dark brown backs. The long, curved bill is well suited to probing deep into flowers for tiny insects and nectar. The exterior of the suspended oval nest is usually so untidy that it gives the impression of a spider's web covering a clump of dead leaves. By contrast, the interior, reached through a side entrance near the top, reveals a neatly-lined chamber. Only the bill of the incubating bird protrudes from the entrance.

Marico Sunbird

Scarlet-chested Sunbird

Red-headed Weaver

Scarlet-chested Sunbird *(Nectarinia senegalensis).* The eye-catching male scarlet-chested sunbird is distinguished from all other sunbirds by his vivid red chest. Identification of females and young is, however, not as easy for they are dowdy, with heavily-spotted upper breasts and chins and dark grey-brown backs. Immature males may have some red on their chests, a sign of their emerging manhood. This species is quite common in the moister areas of the bush-veld, particularly the eastern Transvaal and Zululand. When stands of winter-flowering aloes come into bloom, these sunbirds will travel distances to feast on the nectar which they sip from the bases of flowers, drawing up the sweetness with swift movements of their tongues. Besides nectar, they also feed on small insects and spiders living within the blooms.

Red-headed Weaver *(Anaplectes rubriceps).* The males of this species are distinctive during the summer breeding season as they are the only birds with a red mantle extending over the head and down on to much of the breast. Females are also quite easily recognized, having a yellow wash where breeding males have red. Non-breeding males resemble females. The nest has the basic kidney-shaped design common to those of many weavers, but as the photograph suggests, it is an untidy affair and lacks the characteristic smooth-woven outer surface. Most weavers use strips of green grass for weaving, but this species uses dry twigs. Adding to the scrappy impression are the leaves woven into the roof of the nest as water-proofing. The nest is normally attached to the outer branches of a tree and there is usually only one to a tree. Red-headed weavers are most abundant

Masked Weaver

in the moist bushveld of the Transvaal lowveld and northern Zululand.

Masked Weaver *(Ploceus velatus)*. Whereas some weavers breed in great bustling colonies and others nest singly, the masked weaver falls between with most colonies comprising four to ten nests. The male normally pairs with several females. These polygamous birds compete with other males of the species in attracting females to their territory. To do so they depend on colouring and display to persuade prospective mates of their ability to protect territories with a ready supply of food and, of course, to provide well-constructed nests. Like this bird perched at the centre of his domain, males in breeding plumage are brightly-coloured and, with their plain backs and red eyes, differ from other black-faced weavers. Females, young birds and non-breeding males are much duller and are easily confused with other species which also have yellow-washed underparts and olive-brown backs.

Violet-eared Waxbill *(Uraeginthus granatinus)*. This species is the most colourful of the waxbills frequenting South Africa. It is a tiny bird and adults stand a mere 50 mm tall. The sexes are readily distinguished as the male has darker brown body-feathers, while those of the female are lighter. Young birds resemble the female. As with several other waxbills, it prefers the drier bushveld areas but, unlike some, the violet-eared waxbill does not congregate in large flocks and is usually seen in pairs or small parties. Much of the day is spent hopping around on the ground or in small bushes in the bird's constant search for food. Though small insects are occasionally eaten for their rich protein, the violet-eared waxbill is largely a seed eater. The predominantly dry food yields only a fraction of the liquid required by these and other waxbills and, not surprisingly, they are regular visitors at waterholes. The nest is a loose ball of grass with a side entrance and is usually well concealed and inaccessible within a thorny thicket. Three or four pure white eggs are laid. Quite often, however, the nest contains an additional, virtually identical egg. This is likely to belong to the parasitic shaft-tailed whydah which relies on the violet-eared waxbill to raise its young.

Violet-eared Waxbill

Blue Waxbill

Blue Waxbill *(Uraeginthus angolensis).* Male and female blue waxbills are very similar, but the male (the bird on the right) has a more extensive area of darker blue on the belly. Though most abundant in drier areas, small feeding flocks are a regular sight throughout thorny scrubland when they hop around the grass or bushes in search of seed. The call is a characteristic, but difficult to describe, series of quiet 'weets'. The nest is an untidy ball of dry grass, usually deep within a thicket. It is often built near a wasp's nest and though the purpose is not certain, it does suggest a defence strategy as most prospective predators would be wary of approaching these insects too closely. The eggs are white, and young blue waxbills resemble the duller female.

Golden-breasted Bunting *(Emberiza flaviventris).* With an air of propriety this handsome male perches at the lip of his newly-completed nest, a neat cup of twigs and rootlets. It is usually constructed in a shrub and two or three glossy white eggs, marked with a variety of brown blotches and lines, are laid. The golden-yellow breast make this species easy to spot and identify and, in flight, the white wing bars are most conspicuous. Females are slightly duller than their mates. The song is an unmusical, buzzy, 'chitze . . . chitze . . .', usually delivered from a bush-top or from a position just below the upper foliage of a tree. The golden-breasted bunting is most frequently seen, however, as it walks along the ground, foraging beneath bushes or in thick woodland clearings. The diet consists largely of seeds and small insects.

Golden-breasted Bunting

MOUNTAINOUS AREAS

From the narrow coastal strip rimming much of South Africa, the land rises fairly steeply in one, two or sometimes three parallel rows of jagged peaks and ridges. While many rocky, hilly regions dot the central plains, this broad belt, sweeping up from the southern and eastern Cape through the Free State, Lesotho and Natal, and on into the eastern Transvaal, includes the country's major mountain series. From the earliest times this almost-continuous barrier has presented problems to pioneers, road builders and railwaymen striving for the coast or the hinterland, but to a host of birds, from huge eagles to tiny chats, this rugged terrain is their range.

Birds in most areas simply move horizontally and enjoy relatively stable climatic conditions, but in mountains, where altitude changes rapidly, as does the weather, birds have evolved differently. Those living on steep cliffs, for example, must be able to cover the vertical height of the face; to fly both upwards and downwards with ease and speed. And the same is basically true of birds living on less precipitous slopes. Temperature, and weather generally,

changes rapidly and dramatically in the mountains, and while a few may cope with the vicissitudes of this climate year-round, most birds move to lower regions to escape the freezing winds and snows of winter. Even in the summer, winds funnel through the kloofs and gorges at speed, creating frequent and sudden up- and down-drafts. Birds that spend a lot of time in the air must, therefore, have the strength and flying power to withstand these buffeting air currents.

It is not easy to pin-point the best birding areas in the mountains, and visits to any rocky slope with a good covering of shrubs are likely to be rewarding. Several of the species in this chapter associate with proteas and often occur in large numbers when these shrubs are in bloom. Mountain tops, however, are only worth visiting in high summer, for at other times few birds are likely to be seen.

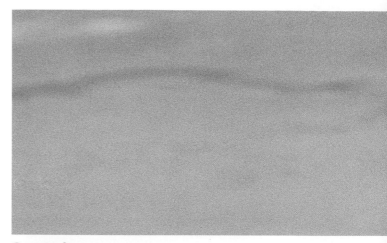

Cape Vulture

Bald Ibis (Geronticus calvus). The bright-red, bald pate of this curiously-impressive bird is most striking and is a characteristic shared only by a closely-related ibis inhabiting North Africa and the Middle East. As with most ibises, the members of this species are commuters, and travel daily between hilly areas and open grasslands. Steep slopes, particularly cliffs rising from rivers, are preferred for breeding and roosting, while open grasslands are combed for insect prey. Once fairly widespread, the bald ibis is today entirely restricted to a narrow strip edging the Drakensberg, Maluti mountains, northern Natal and the eastern Transvaal. Here its range coincides with areas of intense agricultural activity and, consequently, suitable foraging grounds are limited. Not surprisingly, therefore, the bald ibis's somewhat tenuous grip has attracted the close attentions of conservationists. At present the species appears to be in no immediate danger, but this might well change with further in-roads into natural grasslands.

Cape Vulture (Gyps coprotheres). This species is included because it is conspicuous, not because it is common. In fact, the Cape vulture may well be one of the most threatened birds in South Africa. Its natural range closely matches areas of the most intense industrial and agricultural development and, here, the particular needs of this large, specialist scavenger have placed it at a distinct disadvantage. Cape vultures are frequently electrocuted when they attempt to land on electricity pylons, their long wings easily short-circuiting the wires. Many, too, drown while drinking from steep-sided farm reservoirs. Deliberate poisoning by farmers has also taken its toll, but probably the most serious threat is posed by diet deficiencies. Previously, feeding lions, hyenas and other large predators left bone fragments around their kills which scavenging vultures carried to their chicks. With the demise of these carnivores from much of the South African veld, many vulture nestlings lack calcium in their diet. As a result, their bone development is inhibited and, in attempting to fly, these rickety young birds simply topple from their nests. Cape vultures breed in colonies on the ledges of very high cliffs and today the bases of these precipices are often littered with the pathetic remains of calcium-deficient nestlings. A concerned group of people in South Africa police the powerlines and leave piles of bone chips in 'vulture restaurants' in an attempt to reverse the trend.

Bald Ibis

Jackal Buzzard

Rock Kestrel

Jackal Buzzard (*Buteo rufofuscus*). Adults are readily distinguished by their dark, predominantly blue-grey plumages with russet chests. In flight, red-brown tail-feathers and black and white underwings are obvious. Males and females differ only in size, the female being slightly larger than her mate. The largely brown plumage of young birds makes them similar to many eagles and therefore difficult to identify. As with numerous raptors, prey is taken after a rapid downward swoop, either from a high vantage-point or from a hovering position. Mice and other small mammals, reptiles and ground-dwelling insects are all included in the diet. Nests are large, twig platforms built on cliff ledges and are used by the same pair year after year. While their preference for cliff nesting may restrict adults to mountainous regions, where they are indeed common, some young, non-breeding birds move down to lower-lying plains.

Rock Kestrel (*Falco tinnunculus*). Both in Africa and in Europe this species is widely distributed. In Europe it ranges freely in open country, filling a niche similar to that of the black-shouldered kite in Africa. In our part of the world, however, the rock kestrel is mainly confined to hilly regions, perhaps as a result of unsuccessful competition with the 'superior' kite. Though the blue-grey head of many rock kestrels is diagnostic, some specimens have browner heads. This variation is probably related to age and sex, with the immature and young adult females having browner heads than adult males and old females. The rock kestrel frequently hovers as it scans the ground for prey, its wings blurring the air like propellers as it balances the force of gravity. Hovering places great stress on the flight muscles and therefore requires large amounts of energy. This is provided by the high-protein diet of these predatory birds. Hovering is certainly an important element in the feeding strategy of rock kestrels and other raptors as it enables them to hunt in areas devoid of perches. Kestrels do not build nests, instead they use a scrape on a cliff ledge or the old nest of another species.

Black Eagle (*Aquila verreauxii*). One of South Africa's largest and most impressive raptors, the black eagle weighs up to 4,5 kg and stands about 500 mm tall. The jet-black plumage, white 'V' on the back and white patches on the flight feathers of adults are diagnostic of the species. Young birds, however, spend their first four or five years clad in a browny plumage which can lead to confusion with other 'brown eagles'. Black eagles are a common sight in mountains and are present wherever high cliffs and abundant food prevail. The prey of most raptors varies widely, but this species is unusual for its virtual specialization; over 90 percent of the diet consists of dassies (rock-rabbits). From their cliff nests, black eagle pairs preside over domains as vast as 40 – 70 km². The extent of the territory is probably inversely related to the size of the dassie population. The eyrie is usually a huge structure, sometimes two or three metres high, the result of additions year after year. This enormous mound of sticks, poised on a high mountain ledge, represents a substantial resource to black eagles and should it collapse, it is possible that the pair could skip breeding for a year to concentrate on its reconstruction.

Spotted Eagle Owl (*Bubo africanus*). This owl is very common in a number of habitats, but especially in thickly-wooded valleys where it rests up during the day in large trees or among boulders. Eagle owls are larger than other owls and this particular species stands about 400 mm tall. The bright-yellow eyes, barring and spotting on the front, and blotchy back are useful identifying features. The 'ear-like' tufts of feathers on top of the head probably have little to do with hearing. They can, however, be raised or lowered according to 'mood' and lend a cat-like appearance to the head. A wide variety of prey is taken, though in most areas mice and insects predominate in the diet. This owl hunts from high perches, often telegraph poles, from where it swoops down to snatch prey on the ground.

Black Eagle

Spotted Eagle Owl

Black Swift *(Apus barbartus)*. High up on most precipitous rock faces, large numbers of wheeling, dark shapes can often be seen defying gravity in rapid, erratic flights during which collisions always seem imminent. These swirling 'missiles' are likely to be black swifts. With their wholly black and dark-brown plumages and long, pointed wings, they are very similar to other swifts. However, in this species, the upper surfaces of the wings appear paler than the very black mantle. Non-breeding black swifts only visit their cliffs to roost, but in the breeding season, beginning in September, large, loudly-crying flocks arrive to build their nests in any available crevice. At other times, black swifts may be seen flying fast and low over the veld, their large mouths gaping widely as they scoop insects from the air.

Cape Rock-jumper *(Chaetops frenatus)*. Cape rock-jumpers are common in the southern Cape mountains, particularly on rocky slopes. These boldly coloured birds stand about 120 mm tall and can often be seen, characteristically erect on long legs, perching on open rocks. Their longish tails are frequently cocked and fanned to display conspicuous white tips. Females and young birds are similar to the males shown here, but are not as brightly marked. Unlike many mountain birds, Cape rock-jumpers are not strong fliers and much of their time is spent leaping from rock to rock or scratching and digging amongst the rubble for insects. Most Cape rock-jumpers start breeding in the late winter months and their nests are bowls of grass tucked securely under rocks.

Mountain Chat *(Oenanthe monticola)*. With their remark-

Black Swift

Cape Rock-jumper

Sentinel Rock-thrush

able variations in plumage, these small birds pose problems for the birdwatcher. All adult males, like the bird shown here tending his young, have greyish caps and white shoulders, but the rest of the body feathering may range from black to pale grey. Females and young birds are basically dark brown. One constant feature, however, provides some help to the birder; all members of the species have white rumps and outer tail-feathers which are conspicuous in birds put to flight. Mountain chats are most common in dry, hilly country where they spend much of the day hopping around and flying between rocks. They are strongly territorial birds and perch boldly on vantage-points.

Sentinel Rock-thrush *(Monticola explorator)*. This species is common on rocky, grassed slopes. The Sentinel Rock-thrush stands about 100 mm tall on rather long legs, and whereas adult males have blue-grey heads, backs and breasts, those of females and juveniles are speckled brown. In contrast to the uniform underparts of females, however, young birds are also spotted brown and dark grey below. As with most thrushes, this species is largely insectivorous and prey is caught on the ground amongst the grass and rocks. Males are fine songsters and are given to displaying themselves prominently on exposed rocks while uttering clear whistles which carry far across the mountain slopes. The nest, hidden between rocks, is usually a large mound of grass, leaves and roots. A small central cup holds three or four pale, greenish-blue eggs which hatch after about two weeks.

Mountain Chat

Grassbird

Bokmakierie

Grassbird *(Sphenoeacus afer)*. Though common in thickly-grassed valleys, grassbirds are often difficult to spot as they spend much of the day skulking in the rank undergrowth or creeping through the grass in search of insects. From time to time, however, these warblers also perch prominently on exposed grass stalks from where they deliver their characteristic song — a series of short whistles forming a phrase lasting about two seconds. Visually, grassbirds can be recognized by their long scraggy tails and finely-streaked flanks. At close-range, moustache-like black lines can be seen drooping from the corners of the beak. Adults measure about 180 mm from the point of the beak to the tip of the tail and are substantially longer than other warblers and cisticolas occupying similar habitats.

Bokmakierie *(Telophorus zeylonus)*. Translate the syllables of the common name into a sequence of loud whistles and you have a fair imitation of this shrike's typical call — a sound which characterizes a variety of habitats ranging from Karoo scrub to open grassland and mountain slopes. This penetrating song is usually delivered from a prominent perch and an accompaniment may be provided by the mate. The bright yellow underparts and black bib, as well as the dark green back are all diagnostic. In flight, these birds also show distinct yellow ends to their tail feathers. Bokmakieries prey largely on insects, but may take small vertebrates such as lizards and frogs. They spend much of their time rummaging underneath bushes and at times, when running along the ground on their long legs, they look more like resplendently-dressed larks than bush-shrikes.

Red-winged Starling *(Onychognathus morio)*. At a distance, red-winged starlings appear black with reddish-brown wings, but at close range, the largely blue-black body feathers become obvious. With their wings folded, however, little of the characteristic red colour is shown. Adult males have glossy, blue-black heads, while females and immatures have greyish mantles extending down onto their necks. The calls are characteristic 'pee.yoou . . . pee.yoou' whistles. Red-winged starlings often sip nectar from flowers and, in so doing, their heads become dusted with pollen. Moving from flower to flower while feeding in this manner, starlings undoubtedly play an important role in the cross-pollination of flowers. Flocks will often enter built-up areas to raid gardens, and in some heavily-developed regions the species has adapted to nesting in buildings and even mining headgears. These tall structures presumably provide nooks and crannies similar to those in the cliff faces of their natural habitat.

Red-winged Starling

Cape Sugarbird

Gurney's Sugarbird

Cape Sugarbird *(Promerops cafer)*. Visitors to the botanical gardens at Kirstenbosch in Cape Town are likely to see a number of birds resembling giant sunbirds. These are Cape sugarbirds, members of a family probably not even remotely related to the sunbirds. The superficial likeness between these two groups can, however, be explained in terms of convergent evolution, for just as the sunbirds derive nutrition from sipping the nectar of veld flowers, so do the sugarbirds. Sugarbirds have become particularly specialized in that they are almost totally dependent on proteas for their food requirements. Cape sugarbirds are common in the southern Cape mountains from Cape Town eastwards to Ciskei. They are best identified by their long, curved bills, grey-brown backs, dirty-white fronts and long tails. Adults range between 300 and 400 mm in overall length, females having slightly shorter tails than males. During the winter breeding season, male Cape sugarbirds become intensely territorial and reveal themselves to potential spouses and competitors in spectacular display flights, their tails held doubled over their backs and their wings clapping furiously. Nests are cup-shaped bowls of leaves and twigs and are lined with downy material obtained from protea blossoms. A clutch of two eggs is normally laid.

Gurney's Sugarbird *(Promerops gurneyi)*. This species and the Cape sugarbird together comprise the Promeropidae, the only family of birds unique to South Africa. Their evolution and that of the protea are probably closely linked. Gurney's sugarbird is primarily a Drakensberg species, but

Malachite Sunbird

occurs from the eastern Cape to the northern Transvaal. It is found mainly in association with proteas and is most common where good stands of these shrubs are in bloom. In their natural habitat Gurney's sugarbirds move about according to where proteas are flowering, but in some commercial protea nurseries in Natal they have become resident. In the eastern Cape, where the distributions of the two sugarbirds overlap slightly, Gurney's sugarbirds are distinguished by their russet chests and shorter tails. Unlike the Cape sugarbird the members of this species nest in summer from September to February.

Malachite Sunbird (*Nectarinia famosa*). This is another species largely dependent on proteas for food and it is, not surprisingly, particularly common on mountain slopes during summer when these plants flower. During the winter, however, it frequently moves to lower-lying areas to feed on aloe blooms. The plumage of the male shown here is at an intermediate stage between that of the breeding male and that of females, young birds and non-breeding males. Males in full breeding splendour are indeed dazzling; glossy green overall except for a yellow tuft on the shoulder of each wing. This spectacular plumage is a significant factor in the attraction of a mate as females probably select those males with the brightest and neatest plumages. Sleek, handsome males are likely to be well-fed and therefore the occupants and, by implication, the successful defenders of territories with abundant food. Males in tatty plumage on the other hand are unlikely to win mates as they would probably make poor providers.

Orange-breasted Sunbird *(Nectarinia violacea)*. In their breeding plumages the male members of this species are undoubtedly the most colourful of the mountain birds selected for this chapter. Their vivid orange, violet and green colours are quite stunning and are also diagnostic of the species. Females and juveniles, however, are drab, with greenish-yellow undersides and greeny-brown backs. They also lack the elongate central tail feathers of males. Orange-breasted sunbirds are most abundant in the south-western Cape where they associate with proteas and ericas. Their food consists largely of nectar, supplemented with a few insects hawked from the air or gleaned from foliage. Males are particularly conspicuous in the breeding season when they perch prominently on bush-tops while delivering their high-pitched songs. Breeding takes place in the winter months and the nest is usually placed low down, in a bush.

Rock Bunting *(Emberiza tahapisi)*. The characteristic features of this species are the dark-brown body feathering and black and white stripes on the head. Females and young birds, however, have these markings restricted to the sides of the head. While not very obtrusive, rock buntings are quite common in hilly areas with plenty of rocky outcrops. Here small parties often gather on the ground in clearings where they scratch for seeds and small insects. The cup-shaped nests, woven from grass and fine roots, are usually hidden among grass tufts or in the cover of a few rocks. On average, each nest holds a clutch of three eggs which are basically beige, with heavy russet spotting.

Orange-breasted Sunbird

Rock Bunting

COASTS AND ESTUARIES

The South African coastline has an amazingly rich diversity of habitats ranging from rocky shores to sandy beaches, from tidal mudflats and marshes to mangrove thickets and estuaries. Each supports a wide variety of birds and some inhabitants, like the jackass penguin, the bank and Cape comorants and the Cape gannet, are endemic breeders to South Africa. These and other species are permanent residents and remain all year round, but many more are visitors who come to escape the long, rigorous winters that close in on their breeding habitats, and to exploit the bountiful food to be gleaned from both the tidal zone and the deeper offshore waters of our coasts. During the summer months, migrants from the north arrive in countless thou-

sands and with their departure the following autumn, seabirds from the rime-cold wastes of the sub-Antarctic and Antarctic move in to take their place.

Expansive estuaries and the nutrient-rich Benguela Current sweeping up the West Coast make the southern and western shores of South Africa particularly attractive to sea and coastal birds. By contrast, however, the East Coast has very few outstanding estuarine habitats and consequently it supports relatively smaller numbers of birds.

Rocky headlands make good vantage-points for birders to see oceanic birds and the best areas in the Cape include Cape Point, Cape Hangklip and the sewage outflow at Mouille Point. In and around Durban, both the north and

south piers and the Bluff are most rewarding. The majority of estuaries dotted along the coast, harbour an abundance of wading birds, but the finest are the Langebaan Lagoon and the Berg River in the south-western Cape and the Swartkops River near Port Elizabeth. In Natal, the Bayhead Estuary in Durban, though being rapidly reclaimed, still holds many birds, while further north, in Zululand, the Richards Bay Sanctuary and the Tugela River estuary are worth visiting.

Jackass Penguin (*Spheniscus demersus*). This offshore and island-dwelling penguin is usually only seen on the mainland when ill or covered with oil, a depressingly frequent occurrence these days with the many ships discharging their bilges as they round Africa. This is posing a major threat to the survival of South Africa's only breeding penguin. All seabirds are vulnerable to oil pollution, but penguins are especially so as these flightless birds spend the greater part of their lives at sea. Very often the detergents used to control fuel and crude oil pollutants disrupt the delicate structure of penguin plumes. The birds are thus robbed of their waterproofing, a vital element in their defence against the cold of the sea. Waterlogged, they are forced ashore to starve. The situation is exacerbated when the birds, in a futile attempt to clean themselves, swallow lethal amounts of oil. Breeding is confined to the islands of the Cape coast, especially those in the west. Where possible, a pair will excavate a burrow in which two eggs are laid, but on rocky islands devoid of soil they must either nest under rocks or in the open. Penguin eggs, considered a delicacy, were once harvested by the thousand. This practice was responsible for decreased populations which, in view of the added stress caused by pollution, have yet to recover. Fortunately, egg harvesting is now illegal. Jackass penguins derive their common name from their donkey-like braying which, in large colonies, often results in a night-long raucous din.

Black-browed Albatross (*Diomedea melanophris*). Appearing much like a huge kelp gull, this oceanic nomad can be identified by its long, pinkish-orange bill, very broad, black borders to the white underwings and by the stiffly held wings which are rarely flapped when gliding low over the sea. The black-browed albatross breeds on the cold windswept islands of the sub-Antarctic and migrates northwards with the onset of winter. It is by far the most common of the albatrosses visiting South Africa and is regularly seen flying close inshore along the southern Cape. Here the food-rich Benguela Current, and the offal discarded by trawlers, attracts this species and many others in large numbers. Albatrosses are most remarkable for their ability to soar. Though take-off is sometimes long and laboured, once airborne they glide for hours, or even days, with seeming ease. The principles underlying the albatross's soaring flight are quite different from those operating for land birds. Over large expanses of water there are no rising thermals (there is no heat radiating from the water to generate them) and the only air currents are horizontal gusts. Friction with the water slows the air-flow and, as a result, the air speed near the water is slower than at higher levels. Albatrosses use the varying velocities of these air currents to accelerate and to produce 'lift'; their long, narrow, but rigid, wings providing effective, sturdy aerofoils.

Cape Gannet (*Morus capensis*). The Cape gannet shown here descends almost vertically onto its nesting site with great skill. Uncannily, it is guided to the exact spot by the call of its mate or nestlings which can be distinguished from the thousands of 'voices' that 'jam' the colony with a ceaseless cacophony. The bird's fishing prowess, too, is remarkable and a fishing gannet is spectacular to watch as it checks in mid-air, sometimes at a great height, and then plummets head-first into the sea. Much of its food is taken at the surface, but the gannet's dive can carry it more than ten metres deep. To cushion it from the considerable impact on entering the water, the Cape gannet has spongy layers of tissue in the skin covering the head, as well as air pockets in the breast region. The long, thin, black line on the throat, visible in the bird shown in the bottom right corner of the photograph, is in fact a flexible patch of bare skin which expands when a large fish is swallowed. In the dense breeding colonies that envelop small, flat islands each pair occupies an area just big enough to be out of their neighbours' pecking range. Here their nest is built from debris and excrement and a single chalky white egg is laid. The courtship display involves bill fencing, neck entwining and mutual head and neck preening. These elaborate rituals all serve to reinforce the bond between pair members. When flying over the colony and when diving, the call is a loud throaty 'waaarrrah waaarrrah'.

Jackass Penguin

Black-browed Albatross

Cape Gannet

Cape Cormorant

Bank Cormorant

Cape Cormorant *(Phalacrocorax capensis)*. Flying low over the sea in their typical 'V' formations, Cape cormorants are often seen moving from one fishing area to the next. These are the most prolific of the cormorants in South Africa, especially in the western Cape where vast shoals of pelagic fish provide an abundant food source. When a shoal is detected, Cape cormorants gather, literally in their thousands, and the water boils as they dive and leap-frog over one another in pursuit of fish. These gregarious birds also gather in huge numbers to breed. Their ammonia-rich excrement, guano, is prized as fertilizer and each year the cormorants' densely-packed island colonies are visited by labour teams who scrape the guano from the rocks. On some islands, flat, wooden breeding platforms have been constructed to make guano collection easier. This species is smaller and less robust than the bank cormorant, and is distinguished by the yellow patch at the base of its bill.

Bank Cormorant *(Phalacrocorax neglectus)*. In the opening sequence to a rather comical breeding display, the male shown here calls a strident 'wheeeee' as he drops into the colony. As he touches down he will run forward, slapping his large, webbed feet on the rocks, drooping his wings and cocking his tail to expose his white rump. He will then throw his head and neck slightly forward and then backwards over his back and rump. Bank cormorants do not form the vast colonies of other species; instead they breed in small groups

Little Egret

which return to the same rocky outcrop year after year. Despite their social inclinations, bank cormorants have little respect for the property of their fellows and if a pair leave their nest unguarded for even a short period, their immediate neighbours will steal large billfuls of nesting material to add to their own nests. Unlike Cape cormorants, the members of this species do not range far out to sea to feed, but catch small fish and crayfish among the rocks.

Little Egret *(Egretta garzetta)*. Certainly the most active feeder of all the egrets, moments of quiet poise while fishing are few and far between in the life of the little egret. More usually it is dashing restlessly to and fro in shallow water, pursuing prey which includes a wide range of aquatic in-

sects, small fish and frogs. Sometimes, in the middle of its frenetic hunting sorties, the little egret appears to dance with its wings outstretched; in fact it is using its feet to stir the muddy bottom in the hope of disturbing some item of food. Its small size, black legs and yellow feet, conspicuous as the bird 'high-steps' through the water, are all diagnostic of the species. Also characteristic in the breeding season are the attractive, wispy plumes on the head, neck and back. At the turn of the century these plumes were a much sought-after adornment to ladies hats and, like the great white egret, this species was slaughtered in thousands. The little egret breeds in mixed heronries; a flimsy platform is constructed in a tree and four or five white eggs are usually laid.

African Fish Eagle

Greater Flamingo

Lesser Flamingo

Greater Flamingo *(Phoenicopterus ruber)*. The most diagnostic feature of the greater flamingo is the bulbous, down-curved bill which is pink with a dark tip. The lovely, rosy red colour on the forewings is only visible when the birds are flying. Ill-proportioned and somewhat ungainly, the long, sinuous neck and heavy bill, trademarks of all flamingoes, belie their great efficiency. Flamingoes are highly-specialized filter-feeders and when gathering food, as many of the birds shown here are doing, the head is dipped beneath the surface and is agitated by the supple neck. In the process, food-rich, muddy water is drawn into the trough-like lower jaw. By using the tongue to pump out the water, small aquatic animals are trapped in the hairy structures lining the bill. The greater flamingo breeds sporadically in South Africa, in some years nesting in large numbers. Each nest is a flat-topped cone of mud and a single, large white egg is laid.

Lesser Flamingo *(Phoenicopterus minor)*. Lesser flamingoes are easily distinguished from the previous species by their smaller size and very dark, red bill which from a distance appears black. Their body and forewing feathers also tend to be coloured a deeper rosy-red. Sometimes these birds are encountered in their tens of thousands – one of the most impressive birding sights in South Africa. Their calls are goose-like grunts and honks. Lesser flamingoes are mainly summer visitors and with the coming of colder weather they migrate to their central African breeding grounds, though numbers do overwinter in South Africa. As with many gregarious birds that cover great distances on the wing, they fly in large 'V' formations. Energy is thus conserved, as each bird derives 'lift' from his neighbours' slipstream. The lead bird, of course, has to make its own headway and to spread the load the birds constantly rotate position.

African Fish Eagle *(Haliaeetus vocifer)*. Throwing its head upwards and over its back, the fish eagle gives its yelping cry, truly one of the most evocative sounds of Africa. Uttered while perched or in mid-flight, this loud, but beautiful call carries clearly and is well known to anyone familiar with South Africa's lakes and estuaries. This majestic raptor is a superb fisherman. From a perch high above the water, or while flying, it swoops down to pluck its prey from just below the surface. Sometimes, however, when grappling with a particularly large fish, the bird may plunge deep into the water. A few birds have been known to drown in this manner, for they become waterlogged and lack the strength to heave themselves back into the air or paddle to the shore. In addition to the fish eagle's fearsome talons, its soles and toes have special rough scutes which help to grip slippery prey. The nest is a large platform of sticks placed in a tree close to the water's edge. Two or three white eggs are laid.

Black Oystercatcher (*Haematopus moquini*). Watched by his unruffled companion, the black oystercatcher in the foreground excitedly calls 'chepeeep chepeeep'. When really alarmed, however, the cry is reminiscent of the noisy whistle made by a child's squeaky toy. The black oystercatcher is endemic to southern Africa; it is found along the length of the Cape coast, but it is most abundant along the western shores where its range extends northwards to Angola. It does not feed on oysters as its common name implies, instead it forages actively along the water's edge, prising mussels and limpets from the rocks. In its search for food the oystercatcher also probes deep into the sand with its bill in the hope of dislodging some morsel. The nest is a scrape in sand or shingle and two, well marked eggs are laid. Though seldom molested by humans, their presence in

Black Oystercatcher

breeding areas often keeps these birds away from their nests. Without the protection of the parent's body, many eggs overheat in the hot summer sun and the developing embryos die. In unprotected areas, people could, unwittingly, be placing these birds under considerable stress.

Turnstone *(Arenaria interpres)*. This summer visitor to the South African coast arrives in September and departs the following April on its 12 000-km-long return journey to the wastelands of the Arctic tundra. It is easily recognized as it is the only small shore bird with a russet back and a black and white face pattern. The turnstone is often encountered, especially on rocky coastlines, as it scuttles busily along the high-tide mark in its constant search for food. The short, robust, and slightly upturned bill provides an ideal tool for overturning small stones and sorting through debris to glean tiny crustaceans lurking beneath. Turnstones form small flocks and roost in large numbers with other wading birds.

White-fronted Sandplover *(Charadrius marginatus)*. This small plover is commonly seen running swiftly along sandy beaches with its head held low, stopping suddenly and bobbing its head before dashing off again in a different direction. It almost always occurs in pairs, and rarely forms flocks. The white-fronted sandplover feeds on small crustaceans and sand-hoppers, picked from the beach after short, fast spurts across the sand. The call is a soft 'whit whit'. The nest, a mere scrape in the sand, holds two or three sandy coloured eggs which meld effectively with the surrounding sand and shells. For added protection against would be predators, an adult leaving its nest scuffles its feet to hide the eggs under a thin covering of sand.

Turnstone

White-fronted Sandplover

Sanderling

Sanderling *(Calidris alba).* Small flocks of sanderlings frequent sandy beaches where they are a common sight, racing after receding waves, quickly gleaning any exposed morsel before the next incoming wave surges over the feeding area and drives them back up the beach. In these repeated and rather comical, but perfectly-timed, games of tag with the sea, these little birds move with such speed that their legs reduce to a blur. Sanderlings are easily distinguished from white-fronted sandplovers by their larger size, longer bills and greyish, mottled backs. Small populations remain in South Africa during the winter, but sanderlings are largely migratory and those few permanent residents are augmented each spring by the thousands that arrive from their Arctic breeding grounds. Their flight is swift and dashing, with small groups twisting, turning and tumbling through the air continually calling 'cheet cheet'.

Whimbrel *(Numenius phaeopus).* The conspicuously striped crown, downward-curving bill, and white 'V'-shaped rump are characteristic of this large wading bird. The call, a fast, seven-note whistle, is also diagnostic. The whimbrel is generally very alert and nervous, and is easily startled. At the slightest hint of danger it flies off, showing its white rump and shrilling loudly. Feeding as it does along exposed shorelines and mudflats, the whimbrel is exposed to danger from all sides, and the bird's wariness is, therefore, very necessary. The whimbrel is a cosmopolitan species and from its summer nesting quarters in the high latitudes of the north it disperses widely throughout the southern hemisphere to escape the arctic winter.

Avocet *(Recurvirostra avosetta).* The long, thin, upturned bill, clearly visible in the birds shown here, is a most effective adaptation to shallow-water feeding. Sweeping its bill from side to side, the avocet scythes the water just below the surface to pick up small surface animals. The avocet, however, is not confined to feeding in the shallows; by virtue of its partially-webbed feet, the bird is also a fair swimmer and when paddling in deeper water it often dips its head well below the surface, sometimes even 'up-ending' like a duck. When breeding, the avocet forms small, loose colonies. Each nest is a shallow scrape on the ground, lined with dead vegetation. Clutches comprise three or four greenish-grey eggs which are spotted and lined. Adults cooperate to vigorously defend their nests and young, and, irately crying 'cwit. cwit. cwit.', will mob any intruder. Individuals will also pretend injury in a ruse to draw a potential predator away from their nests.

Avocet

Whimbrel

Kelp Gull

Stilt

Stilt *(Himantopus himantopus).* Unmistakable with its black back and wings and extra-long, red legs, this 'elevated' wading bird is able to feed in deeper water than its shorter-legged rivals. When feeding in water, the stilt simply dips its bill to snatch insects or larvae from the surface, but to pick up food on dry land, the bird is forced to flex its long legs. Like the whimbrel, the stilt is always on the alert, nervously casting about for approaching danger. At the slightest provocation it will take flight, yelping its loud 'kyick kyick' call. Four eggs are usually laid in a small, flat, grass nest which is placed on marshy ground or floating vegetation. The incubating adult is literally 'all legs' as it struggles to bend its lanky limbs and manoeuvre its body over the eggs.

Kelp Gull *(Larus dominicanus).* Riding an air current with practised ease, the kelp gulls shown here leisurely scan the coastline, ever watchful for a meal. These large black and white gulls with heavy, yellow and orange bills are the major predators in the seabird colonies of the Cape. They will often use high boulders as vantage-points to watch over a colony and are quick to swoop down on any unguarded egg or chick. The colonies of other gulls, penguins, terns and cormorants are all regularly raided, and even in their own nesting colonies, kelp gulls are not averse to robbing their neighbours' nests. These gulls are also particularly partial to mussels, but though able to prise them from the rocks, their beaks lack the power to crush these hard shells. Therefore, to break the mussels open, they fly up and drop them onto a suitable rock. Some gulls use this technique with great finesse. Breeding begins in October and the kelp gulls' large nesting colonies are usually located on offshore islands. Immature kelp gulls are very different from adults and are mottled brown and white with black bills.

Hartlaub's Gull *(Larus hartlaubii).* This gull is common only along the coast from Cape Agulhas to the western Cape. It seldom strays far inland, but occasionally it visits coastal farms where it follows tractors to feast on grubs and worms unearthed by the plough. It is a notorious scavenger; it feeds voraciously on the offal discarded in fishing harbours, scrounges around rubbish dumps and gleans scraps at drive-in restaurants around Cape Town. Dense breeding colonies form on offshore islands, and recently this gull has started to nest on flat-topped buildings along the Cape Town seafront. Crammed almost on top of one another, nests are jumbled collections of dead vegetation and debris.

Hartlaub's Gull

Swift Tern

Common Tern

Common Tern *(Sterna hirundo)*. The birds shown here wear their non-breeding plumage and, being visitors only, they rarely treat birders in South Africa to the handsome breeding dress sported in the northern hemisphere. Common terns arrive in September and spend the summer along our coasts where they are often encountered in flocks of countless thousands. Wheeling and twirling like huge clouds of down driven before a gust of wind, these flocks follow small offshore shoaling fish. Most prey is simply picked from the surface or taken in a shallow dive. Common terns rarely settle on the sea to swim, but regularly bathe in the relatively fresh water of river estuaries. They defend their breeding colonies violently and rent the air with angry screams at any intrusion. In South Africa, however, non-breeding terns are not as aggressive and their vocal clamour is reduced to a short and infrequently uttered 'chiit chiit'.

Swift Tern *(Sterna bergii)*. This large, powerfully-built tern is easily identified by its long, yellow bill and black or grizzled cap. It feeds on fish by plunging into the sea from great heights. Courtship displays include graceful airborne manoeuvres with both birds climbing almost out of sight and then drifting downwards in a slow, wavering flight. In these leisurely descents, the one bird follows its mate, repeating each delicate movement as if indulging in some game of aerial 'follow-my-leader'. The call is a harsh 'kerrak kerrak'. Densely-packed breeding colonies form in summer, sometimes in association with Hartlaub's gulls. Each pair lays one egg which rests on the bare ground.

DRY WESTERN AREAS

Flat desert and semi-desert, punctuated occasionally with rocky outcrops and koppies, encroaches on large areas of the Cape, south-western Transvaal and the Orange Free State. In this harsh, moisture-sapping environment, heat and ever-threatening drought, allow only sparse, thorny scrub and grass to grow, with a few acacias here and there lifting their spiky canopies two or three metres off the ground.

As uninviting as it may seem, many birds have come to terms with this sere region. In so doing they have evolved various strategies to cope with such environmental problems as heat stress, the absence of predictable food sources and the lack of adequate cover. One problem above all others, however, tests the adaptive powers of these birds: the lack of water. All successful desert-dwelling birds contend with this constant hazard by retaining as much liquid as possible within their bodies. Some birds survive without ever drinking. These obtain sufficient moisture for their meagre needs either from the meat or fruit they eat, or from

water produced internally as a by-product of their body metabolism. Many other birds simply have to drink regularly. These 'drinkers' must organize their daily 'timetables' with great precision to commute between their roosting or nesting sites and localized water sources such as pans, water-holes and farm dams. These distances are often considerable and much time and energy is taken up with travelling.

There are a number of good birding areas in typical, dry west habitat to the north of Cape Town, many of which are within the scope of a day or a weekend trip. The Kalahari National Park, especially around water-holes, is most rewarding, while there are several regions near Kimberley well worth a visit.

African Shelduck

African Shelduck *(Tadorna cana)*. The male African shelduck has an all-grey head, whereas that of the female is slightly darker. The female also has a white face-patch, a feature which may lead to confusion with the white-faced whistling duck. In flight, both sexes reveal a conspicuous broad expanse of white across the forewings. The African shelduck has a predeliction for foraging in fields of newly-planted crops. Out of the breeding season when large flocks congregate, sometimes comprising hundreds of individuals, real damage can result in cultivated regions, much to the understandable ire of farmers. Shallow dams and muddy vleis are preferred habitats, but unlike any other duck in South Africa, the nest is often placed far from water, deep within the disused tunnel of a burrowing mammal. Aardvark holes are especially favoured. The nest itself is a mat of grass lined with down from the female's breast. As many as ten large, white eggs are laid.

Pygmy Falcon *(Polihierax semitorquatus)*. This, the smallest bird of prey in Africa, weighs only 60-70 g and measures little more than 150 mm from beak to tail-tip. In overall appearance, the pygmy falcon is more like a shrike than a falcon, especially when seen perched along telephone lines. Unusual among birds of prey, males and females are coloured differently; females are chestnut, while the male plumage includes a grey back. A further peculiarity of this species is its habit of taking up residency in a social weaver colony, the presence of a pair and their offspring being betrayed by a white rim of droppings at the entrance to the nest chamber. These uninvited tenants pose little threat to the weavers as the pygmy falcon's prey consists largely of insects and small lizards.

Lanner *(Falco biarmicus)*. While lanners frequent almost every habitat in South Africa, they are particularly common in the drier areas of the country. The heavily streaked front of the bird shown here, identifies it as an immature bird and contrasts with the uniformly unmarked, pinkish-beige breast of adults. Lanners usually breed on cliffs, but in some areas they have taken to breeding on pylons, buildings and in trees. Like all falcons, they do not build their own nests and either use the vacated nests of other species, or merely lay their eggs in a shallow scrape on a cliff ledge. Prey consists largely of birds up to the size of pigeons and small francolins. Queleas are also frequently harassed by lanners who are quick to snatch birds that separate from the safety of their densely-packed flocks. Lanners occasionally also feed on termites, rodents and lizards. Capable of great speed in the air, these predators kill most of their bird prey on the wing after magnificent swoops during which they may reach speeds of 100 km/hour.

Pygmy Falcon

Lanner

Pale Chanting Goshawk

Pale Chanting Goshawk *(Melierax canorus).* Conspicuous and common, these northern Cape birds are often seen perched atop telephone poles lining endlessly straight roads. Chanting goshawks are about 500 mm tall and their pale-grey plumage and long red legs are obvious diagnostic features. The young members of this species wear a different dress, with the grey of the adult being exchanged for various shades of light brown. Plumage patterns, however, are constant for both sexes and all ages; uniform breasts and backs, and barred bellies. Chanting goshawks prey on lizards, small mammals and birds, and while much is stalked on the ground, these raptors are equally capable of dashing aerial chases. Nests are usually stick platforms in large trees. The two greenish-white eggs are incubated by the female who is supplied with food throughout the nesting period by her attentive mate.

Steppe Buzzard *(Buteo buteo).* Migrating southwards to escape the harsh snows that blanket their steppe-land breeding grounds in eastern Europe and Asia, these appropriately-named raptors arrive each October and November. Thousands sojourn in South Africa and though particularly common in the dry winter-rainfall regions of the southern Cape, they are just as likely to be seen in the eastern Transvaal forests or the grasslands of the Orange Free State. Numerous large brown buzzards, eagles and hawks inhabit South Africa and, as the specimen here perched in a wattle tree demonstrates, the steppe buzzard is yet another. This can make identification difficult, but white or pale chest bands, though partially obscured in this side-on view, are usually obvious. The bare lower-legs contrast with the feathered shanks of most eagles and also aid recognition. Prey consists mainly of small mammals and ground-dwelling birds, captured after low, coursing flights from look-outs such as telephone poles and fence posts.

Steppe Buzzard

Fawn-coloured Lark (*Mirafra africanoides*). Larks, like the cisticolas, are drab, nondescript birds and, except when singing or displaying, individual species are extremely difficult to distinguish. Visual recognition of the fawn-coloured lark is particularly difficult, as although the general colouration is tawny, with pale, sometimes lightly-streaked underparts, several sub-species exist, all of which exhibit plumage variations. All the larks, however, have evolved distinctive songs and displays without which individual members of species would, themselves, no doubt be hard-put to recognize one another. It is during the breeding season, when these songs and displays are most evident that the birder stands the best chance of a certain identification. The fawn-coloured lark is most common in the Kalahari thornveld where it is often seen perched on top of a small bush while uttering its short musical song 'cheetee. tee. ree. tee. tee'. The nest, a neat dome, is well hidden under a tuft of grass.

Double-banded Courser (*Rhinoptilus africanus*). When standing still or sitting, the double-banded courser is often difficult to spot, its mottled back blending effectively with the sandy background of its habitat. Once located, however, this long-legged bird with its large head and two black breast-bands, is easily recognized. Reluctant fliers, double-banded coursers scurry around on the ground, usually in pairs or small parties which, even when approached, prefer to dash off swiftly until reaching a safe distance. When sufficiently alarmed, however, they will take to the air at great speed, zig-zagging to and fro while calling a thin 'pee pee'. No attempt is made to construct a nest; the single egg rests on the bare ground, well camouflaged by its buffy colour, streaked with brown and grey.

Swallow-tailed Bee-eater (*Merops hirundineus*). The bright blue, deeply-forked tail is the most obvious diagnostic feature of this species, while the short 'chewit...chewit' call is

Fawn-coloured Lark

Double-banded Courser

Swallow-tailed Bee-eater

also distinctive. The swallow-tailed bee-eater is most often seen perching on telephone wires along roadsides. Such high vantage-points provide unobscured views of the surrounding terrain, and are favoured look-outs from where these bee-eaters launch forays after flying insects. Quite unafraid of man, the members of this species will very often allow close approach. This boldness does not necessarily make the birder's task easy, however, for these restless birds are continually hawking after grasshoppers, wasps and other insects that happen to fly within range. Some bee-eaters form large breeding colonies, but the swallow-tailed bee-eater nests in solitary pairs. A sandy bank or a donga is usually chosen as the nesting site and a long narrow tunnel is excavated. The eggs are laid in a shallow basin at the tunnel's end.

Namaqua Sandgrouse (*Pterocles namaqua*). Namaqua sandgrouse live mainly in the arid wastes of the Kalahari desert

Namaqua Dove

where they feed on dry seeds. Therefore, to obtain water, they undertake daily journeys of as much as 50 km to the nearest water-holes. Taking advantage of the cooler times of the day to make their drinking trips, hundreds of sandgrouse invade these scattered watering points early each morning and again in the late afternoon. These *en masse* and regular-as-clockwork drinking habits make them vulnerable to predators. However, they do not all drink simultaneously and there are usually sufficient sentinels to give early warning of approaching danger. These considerable, twice-daily trips are beyond the ability of young sandgrouse and adults have evolved a remarkable method of carrying water to their nestlings. Wading into the water, their highly absorbant breast-feathers sponge up substantial amounts of liquid and even after their fast return flights through the dry desert air, an amazing quantity of moisture is retained. By nibbling at this sodden mass, nestlings are able to sip sufficient liquid for their needs. Namaqua sandgrouse are also able to withstand very high temperatures. Little attempt is made to lay their eggs in shade and incubating birds are exposed to the full heat of the sun, with temperatures often ranging between 40 and 50 °C. The sexes are clearly differentiated; females are streaked while males have obvious black and white breast-bands.

Namaqua Dove (*Oena capensis*). This is the only South African dove species in which males and females differ markedly in colour. The male, like the bird shown here, has a black bib and a long, dark tail, while the female has a pale chest and a short tail. Young birds resemble females, but are barred below. The Namaqua dove has a distinctive, yet modest and difficult-to-locate, 'hoop...hoop' call. It is usually seen perching low in a bush, or walking on the ground with its shoulders characteristically hunched as it searches for seeds. The nest, a twig platform, is normally built in a low shrub, though it may be placed just above the ground on matted grass. Two pale cream eggs are laid. Males and females take turns at incubating, the rest of the day being taken up searching for seeds or resting up in the quiet shade of a bush.

Namaqua Sandgrouse

Karoo Prinia

Black-chested Prinia *(Prinia flavicans)*. These comical little birds with tails that seem far too long for their short, squat bodies, are common residents of acacia and other scrub thickets. The black chest-band worn by both males and females is distinctive, but this feathering may be lost during winter when the non-breeding adults would resemble their immature pale-fronted offspring. Prinias feed among bushes and occasionally hop around on the ground in their almost-continuous search for insects. The black-chested prinia shown here has found a thick wattle copse suitable for its breeding site, but the ball-like nests of woven grass are more usually hidden in dense clumps of weeds or grass. The basic colour of the eggs varies between blue and brown; each is adorned with dark-brown blotches and scrolling.

Karoo Prinia *(Prinia maculosa)*. The distinctive features of this small warbler are its spotted breast and very long tail, which in adults represents half the body length. Karoo prinias are usually seen hopping through tangled scrub, endlessly searching for food. These birds feed entirely on small insects and, to meet their energy demands, vast numbers are consumed daily. These busy little desert dwellers seldom seem to rest and the birder is often frustrated in his attempts to obtain good views. Karoo prinias are certainly not shy, however, and will boldly hop to a bush-top to scold an intruder or potential predator. When alarmed, these plucky birds cock their tails almost vertically and call loudly, their admonishing cries quite often attracting other birds to the source of discontent.

Pale-winged Starling *(Onychognathus nabouroup)*. Many birds of the more tropical and lushly-vegetated eastern regions of South Africa have closely-related 'sister species' in the dry west. This is certainly the case with red-winged starlings whose western counterparts are the members of this species. The pale, almost-white, 'windows' on the wings of these starlings are distinctive and most conspicuous when the birds are in flight. Males and females are alike, and adults measure about 270 mm in length. The call is a series of plaintive whistles, 'tee.tyoo...tee.tyoo...'. Pale-winged starlings are most commonly seen in small groups, especially in rocky areas. Nests are securely wedged in rock crevices and the shallow cup of twigs usually holds a clutch of three or four greenish-blue eggs.

Black-chested Prinia

Pale-winged Starling

Scaly-feathered Finch

Sociable Weaver

Dusky Sunbird

Dusky Sunbird *(Nectarinia fusca)*. The male shown here proclaims his territory by perching prominently and 'singing' his unmusical, yet distinctive, 'dissr kek kek'. This common sunbird of the dry, northern Cape scrubland is easily identified by its dusky-black plumage and thin, down-curved beak. It is especially abundant in regions where aloes are in bloom. Though it feeds primarily on nectar, as its specialized bill and fondness for aloes suggest, the dusky sunbird also gleans insects from branches and leaves and, like a flycatcher, will even take them in mid-air. The nest is a small untidy bundle of dried grasses and leaves slung from the outer branches of a small bush. The three, small, white eggs are incubated by the female.

Scaly-feathered Finch *(Sporopipes squamifrons)*. This waxbill-sized seed-eater is an amusing little bird, its prominent moustaches reminiscent of those sported by the villain in some Victorian melodrama. It is a common resident of dry country, where it is often seen in small foraging parties on the ground. Obtaining sufficient liquid is often a problem for desert birds and a range of adaptations has evolved to cope with this environmental hazard. Some species, like the double-banded sandgrouse, commute great distances to water-holes and are able to carry water back to their nestlings, while others, like some kingfishers, derive sufficient moisture from the body fluids of their prey. Finches eat mainly dry grass seeds and their ability to thrive for several weeks, if not indefinitely, without drinking water seems to defy the laws of nature. What happens in effect, is that water is produced internally as a by-product in the metabolic breakdown of its food. The retention of this 'metabolic water' is well developed in seed-eaters, though given the opportunity, all these birds will also readily drink water.

Sociable Weaver *(Philetairus socius)*. A fair number of bird species are gregarious, especially during the breeding season when individuals often place their nests very close together. Sociable weavers have adopted this breeding strategy to a unique degree; these birds build massive nest structures, some as much as three metres across and two metres high. Each of these 'condominiums' houses dozens of pairs, all with their own individual nest chambers which are accessed through separate entrances on the underside of the main structure. Though these bustling colonies with their continuous comings and goings often give the impression of something approaching chaos, each has a rigidly ordered social structure. The overall nest in fact comprises several well-defined sub-colonies and the members of one do not infringe the territory of another. Most small birds build new nests every breeding season, but this would obviously be impossible for social weavers. Their colonies, therefore, represent considerable investments, and a great deal of time and effort is expended repairing and adding to them all year round. Some nests are known to have remained in continuous use for more than a century. The colonies are frequently visited by a number of uninvited guests, the most feared being the cobra which systematically glides from chamber to chamber robbing each of its eggs or young. Other animals that find uses for these structures include the giant eagle owl which builds its nest on top and pygmy falcons and rosy-faced love birds which actually co-opt nest chambers for breeding and roosting. In times of drought, farmers may even pull down these considerable bundles of hay for use as cattle fodder.

Black-cheeked Waxbill

Black-headed Canary

Black-cheeked Waxbill *(Estrilda erythronotos)*. Though not the most colourful of the waxbills found in South Africa, if viewed at close range, the fine, delicate barring on its back and breast, together with its reddish flanks and rump, make this an attractive bird. The black face-patch is diagnostic. Black-cheeked waxbills are usually seen in small flocks, either scuffling busily on the ground while searching for insects or, as the bird here demonstrates, perching on grass stems while extracting seeds. Their call note is a soft 'chooee chooee'. For such small birds, their nests are large, and these roughly-woven domes of grass are usually placed high in a thorn tree.

Shaft-tailed Whydah *(Vidua regia)*. Only males in their breeding dress wear wispy 200-mm-long central tail-feathers such as those trailed by the handsome specimen shown here. In this splendid plumage they perform short aerial displays, bouncing and bobbing to attract the attention of females. Judging from their entourages, these rather ungainly manoeuvres are largely successful and though not proven, each male is thought to have more than one mate. Shaft-tailed whydahs do not make their own nests. Instead, like the members of the cuckoo family, each female lays her single egg in the nest of another bird. Violet-eared waxbills appear to be the birds exploited in this manner by shaft-tailed whydahs, but other waxbills may also be used. Upon hatching, the baby whydahs, unlike cuckoo young, do not eject their nest companions and are raised in harmony with them until they all fledge. Out of the breeding season, shaft-tailed whydahs gather in large flocks, often seen as they forage on the ground for seeds and insects.

Black-headed Canary *(Serinus alario)*. With their chestnut backs and black heads and bibs, the adult males of this species are very distinctive. Females are also easily recognized, for although the black head and bib is lacking, they too have characteristic chestnut backs. Black-headed canaries form small flocks which occasionally associate with larger flocks of seed-eaters, especially the yellow canary. These large gatherings are most prevalent when great areas of the grasses on which they feed are in seed. The call is a soft 'chwee chwee', but males also deliver a short melodious chirping song as part of their breeding display. The small, cup-shaped nests are woven from fine grasses and placed low in a bush, but rarely on the ground. Four or five eggs are laid. In dry regions, breeding commences with the onset of rains. This strategy is employed by a number of species in the dry west, as by the time the eggs hatch, the much-needed moisture has had its effect – plants and insects proliferate and for a short while at least, food is abundant.

Shaft-tailed Whydah

Yellow Canary

Yellow Canary *(Serinus flaviventris)*. The males of this species are the brightest yellow of all the canaries found in South Africa. Females, however, are duller, with finely-streaked breasts. Yellow canaries are commonly seen in small groups and family parties, sometimes in association with the members of the previous species, as they scratch for seeds and small insects on the ground. Males become intensely territorial during the nesting season and from exposed perches within their domains, pour forth a fine melodic song equal to that of any caged, domestic canary. Nests are similar to those of black-headed canaries, but are larger and in addition, small twigs are used to form a sturdy base. Four eggs are laid which take 12 days to hatch. The nestlings are fed on a variety of small insects.

Lark-like Bunting *(Emberiza impetuani)*. This is undoubtedly one of the drabbest bird species in South Africa. Individuals are uniformly fawn-coloured and have no distinctive plumage patterns. Though understandably difficult to identify, with practise the observer will learn to recognize the general shape and posture of these birds. Their movements from one feeding area to another are very rapid and unpredictable. In some cases, however, their abundance is linked to rainfall, for wherever 'downpours' have nourished substantial crops of grass seed, lark-like buntings are extremely common. Breeding, too, may occur suddenly, probably also associated with food supply, and an area will rapidly become alive with males singing heartily from bush-tops and other raised points. Nests are shallow cups on the ground and here the nondescript plumage comes into its own, for incubating birds are well camouflaged against the dull sandy colours of their surroundings.

Lark-like Bunting

EVERGREEN FORESTS

Natural evergreen forests should not be confused with the vast pine and eucalyptus plantations that blanket over one million hectares of South Africa's countryside. The ten million cubic metres of timber yielded each year by these plantations are of undisputed importance in terms of the economy, but they hold little wealth in terms of their fauna. Contrasting sharply with these uniform, largely sterile environments devoid of undergrowth, natural forests, which cover only a fraction of the country's surface, teem with life. Here amongst the large and small trees of many different species, birds thrive. These trees, festooned with tangled vines and creepers trailing down into a thick and often im-

penetrable undergrowth, provide not only shelter and nesting sites, but also an all-year abundance of flowers and insects.

Two forest types are found in South Africa, both restricted to high rainfall areas. Humid, hot forests are confined to the sub-tropical Natal coastal belt and river banks in the Transvaal, while cooler deciduous forests are found in the temperate regions of the Cape, the Natal midlands and the eastern Transvaal escarpment.

Birding in a forest can be frustrating, for despite their considerable numbers, forest species tend to skulk in thick cover or to move away when disturbed. Anyone crashing

through the undergrowth and holding loud conversation with companions will see very little. The birder who finds a shady glade and sits quietly, however, will probably see an amazing number of species within a short time. If luck prevails, the patient observer may even witness a 'bird party' — birds of various species in a loose group which glean fruit and insects as they pass systematically through the trees.

Coastal forests worth visiting in Zululand are Maplelane at the Mfolozi River mouth and Cape Vidal on the eastern shores of Lake St Lucia. The Natal midlands include many patches of natural forest, the most accessible being Town Bush in Pietermaritzburg and the Weza Forest near Umzimkulu. Along the Garden Route the famous Knysna and Tsitsikama forests certainly merit a visit. In the Transvaal, the extensive Woodbush Forest near Tzaneen provides sanctuary for some rare forest species. The small patches of forest in the Zoutpansberg near Louis Trichardt, however, are perhaps the most rewarding of all, for here can be found all the species mentioned in this chapter — and a whole lot more besides.

Long-crested Eagle *(Lophaetus occipitalis)*. This small, dark eagle is easily recognized by its long, wispy crest and white-feathered legs. In flight, the white bases of the wing feathers and the black and white barred tail are also conspicuous. It is one of the few forest birds that has adapted to eucalyptus and pine plantations. Here it is frequently seen, sitting motionless on an exposed perch at the plantation edge. Dead trees are particularly favoured as look-outs, for their leafless branches allow a clear view while the bird scans the ground for prey. In natural forests, the long-crested eagle behaves in much the same way; it favours swampy areas along forest borders where it hunts by swooping down from a high perch to snatch its prey on the ground. Small rodents,

Long-crested Eagle

Hadeda Ibis

Crowned Eagle

reptiles and, occasionally, snakes are eaten. Like all raptors this eagle is strongly territorial and pairs are often seen swirling high in the early morning air as they patrol their domains. The call is a plaintive 'whee-aah whee-aah'.

Hadeda Ibis *(Bostrychia hagedash).* Like all ibises, the members of this species commute fair distances each day to reach their feeding grounds. When flying to and from their roosts very early in the morning, or late in the evening, the loud, deep 'ha, ha . . . ha, ha' calls of these woodland ibises carry clearly on the still air. Indeed, these are probably amongst the most familiar and most distinctive of the bird calls heard around the forested areas of South Africa. The hadeda ibis has an overall brown plumage with a dark, bronze patch on each forewing and a pale, creamy stripe below each eye. The dark, down-curved bill with a bright red central stripe along the top, is also diagnostic. A wide variety of insects is eaten. Prey is usually picked from the forest floor, or, as shown here, when striding across open terrain. Unlike other, more social ibises, the hadeda nests in single pairs high in the outer branches of tall trees. The nest itself is a large stick platform.

Crowned Eagle *(Stephanoaetus coronatus).* Though not the largest of the African raptors, the crowned eagle is certainly the most powerful. Monkeys and dassies are the most common items on its menu, but it is also known to take on, and overcome, animals as large as antelope. It is certainly a most efficient killing machine and animals seized in its large, extremely powerful talons have little prospect of reprieve, soon being despatched in their vice-like grip. Pairs are thought to hunt together and to have evolved a highly effective *modus operandi;* one bird provides a decoy by distracting the potential victim while its mate strikes unseen to make the kill. The crowned eagle is identified by its large size, broad, rounded wings and the heavy, rufous barring on the belly and underwings. As illustrated here, the nest is a colossal affair of branches and twigs. The structure is used year after year by the same pair. Though two eggs are laid, only one chick survives. This is the result of a struggle between the two siblings which ultimately results in the death of the weaker. The eagles can probably only feed a single chick, but two eggs are laid to increase the chance of successful breeding should one egg fail to hatch. In a spectacular territorial display over the forest canopy, both birds rise steeply to a considerable height and then swoop down swiftly, only to rise again to repeat the manoeuvre. Throughout the display, the birds call a high-pitched 'keeype keeype'.

African Goshawk *(Accipiter tachiro)*. This large, long-tailed hawk with its distinctive, rounded wings, is often seen circling above the forest in the early morning. During these daybreak displays it continually calls a soft 'chrup chrup'. When hunting, however, it flies low down, speedily negotiating its way through forests or patrolling their perimeters. In these dashes it often surprises small birds, catching them after a short chase which sometimes ends with both predator and victim crashing through the forest undergrowth. The African goshawk's feet are fearsome weapons; its toes are long and thin, and armed with needle-sharp claws which make short work of animals 'stapled' in their powerful grip. Males are noticeably smaller than females who are able to store large fat and protein reserves to help withstand occasional food shortages. Males, however, have greater aerial agility and the ability to out-manoeuvre small prey. Thus a pair of African goshawks is able to exploit a wide range of prey, with the male taking small animals and leaving larger ones to his mate.

Green Pigeon *(Treron calva)*. The bright yellow and green plumage worn by the members of this species is diagnostic. This does not necessarily make the birder's task easy, however, for these colours provide an excellent camouflage in the dappled light high in a leafy canopy. Green pigeons often occur in large numbers, especially when wild figs are ripe. They are active feeders and clamber, parrot-like, through the tangled mass of branches and leaves. Sometimes, as the bird here demonstrates, they even hang upside-down to reach and tear open ripe fruit. It is during these moments of high feasting that the observer is likely to be rewarded, not only with views of this pigeon, but also of a number of other species that join with it to exploit the food bounty. The nest – a rough platform of twigs – is typical of those of most doves and pigeons. Two glossy white eggs are laid. When newly-hatched, the young are virtually naked, having only a slight covering of fluffy down.

Knysna Loerie *(Tauraco corythaix)*. These lovely birds are usually seen bounding from branch to branch, their crimson primary wing-feathers flashing brightly. Their loud, raucous 'kow kow kow' cries carry far throughout the forest. The alarm note, a gurgled hissing sound, is strangely quiet by comparison. Knysna loeries are continuously on the move, usually as members of small parties, as they search for food. They are often found feeding alongside green pigeons and trumpeter hornbills in wild fig trees. Nests are small twig platforms placed high in a tree. Each nest usually contains two white eggs. Immature birds resemble their parents, but have less red on their wings.

African Goshawk

Green Pigeon

Knysna Loerie

Black-headed Oriole

Black-headed Oriole (*Oriolus larvatus*). The black head and pink bill of this strikingly-coloured bird are unmistakable. Immature birds resemble their parents, but have dark heads flecked with buff and streaked breasts. When feeding on nectar as the black-headed oriole shown here is doing, the bill and face often become discoloured by the bright yellow pollen. This can be confusing when trying to identify the bird, especially when it is seen at a distance. Nectar, however, constitutes only a small part of the diet, most of this oriole's nourishment being derived from berries and insects. The call is a very loud, but liquid, 'cheoop, cheoop' which carries clearly even in very dense cover. The nest is a neatly constructed hammock of long, stringy lichens bound by cobwebs. It is slung from a slender branch high in the outer reaches of a tree.

Trumpeter Hornbill

Burchell's Coucal (*Centropus superciliosus*). The individual shown here has an overall dark cap, but some members of the species have white eyebrows, a feature which has given rise to the alternative common name of the white-browed coucal. Burchell's coucal is usually encountered along the forest edge, especially in damp areas, near streams. It spends the majority of its time skulking in the thick vegetation of these regions. The best chance of a good sighting, therefore, is in the early morning when it often suns itself on exposed branches or grass stems. The call is very familiar as well as being diagnostic. It comprises a series of hollow sounding notes 'doe doe doe doe', descending in scale, but rising slightly at the end. This liquid call is frequently heard just before or just after a rainstorm and in some areas the bird is known appropriately as 'the rain bird'. Burchell's coucal feeds on insects, lizards and, sometimes, on the eggs and young of smaller birds.

Trumpeter Hornbill (*Bycanistes bucinator*). The members of this species are often seen in the company of green pigeons as they feed together in the high branches of fig trees. The bird shown here is either a young male or a female as the cask on top of the bill lacks the full development of those displayed by adult males. The highly characteristic, mewing trumpet calls of these birds carry far throughout the thick forest; the hollow bill cask may act as a resonating chamber to amplify the sound. As with other hornbills, the breeding biology of this species is unusual. A large cavity in a tree or cliff is chosen as the nest site and with the female ensconced and ready to lay her eggs, her mate proceeds to seal her in, using a cement of mud and excrement. Only a narrow slit is left through which the male feeds the incubating female and later the nestlings. When the young are nearly ready to fledge, the female ends this period of protective custody by breaking the seal with her powerful bill.

Burchell's Coucal

Sombre Bulbul

Sombre Bulbul *(Andropadus importunus)*. Though the most common of the forest bulbuls, the sombre bulbul is not always obvious. This unobtrusive bird 'hides' in the canopy foliage and when moving around, always manages to keep a leafy sprig between it and the observer. Very often, the only clue to its presence is its characteristic 'willeee willeee' call. When glimpsed, however, the dull, olive back, the pale, yellow-washed underparts and the gleaming, pale eyes, well shown here, confirm correct identification. Fruit and insects make up the bulk of the sombre bulbul's diet and these are taken without fuss as the bird creeps quietly through the foliage. The tiny nest is placed in a small tree or bush. Two eggs are laid and take approximately 15 days to hatch. Though unable to fly, the young leave the nest to clamber through the nest tree within two weeks of hatching.

Natal Robin *(Cossypha natalensis)*. The russet-red underparts and the delicate, powder-blue wings are the most distinguishing features of this robin. In some Natal towns it has become a tame garden inhabitant and will boldly venture out to feed in the open. In the thick forest greenery of its natural habitat, this robin is far more secretive and is exceedingly difficult to spot as it keeps well hidden in the rank undergrowth. In the twilight of morning and evening, however, it becomes more active and conspicuous as it flits from deep cover to forage in the open. The Natal robin has exceptionally large eyes and though not proven, this probably indicates superior vision in low light levels. This would undoubtedly be an advantage in view of its habits of scratching round in the dark undergrowth and hunting in the half-light of dawn and dusk. The call is a soft 'see-saw see-saw', while the song is a spontaneous and pretty melody of jumbled notes and mimicked songs and calls of other forest birds. Two or three eggs are laid in a nest well concealed in a rock crevice or hollow tree stump.

Natal Robin

Bar-throated Apalis

Collared Sunbird

Boubou Shrike

Puff-back Shrike

Boubou Shrike *(Laniarius ferrugineus)*. The common name 'bou bou' is a fairly accurate imitation of this bird's call. This distinctive sound takes the form of a duet, with one bird calling 'boo boo' and its mate answering with a higher-pitched 'tooee'. Variations on these calls are common, however, and they also change from one region to another. The boubou superficially resembles the fiscal shrike, but its tail is shorter and it very rarely if ever, flaunts itself on an exposed perch as does the fiscal. The boubou shrike is, in fact,

very shy and most of the time it skulks in thick vegetation where it also builds its nest. Each brood usually comprises three chicks which after hatching take approximately 16 days to fledge.

Puff-back Shrike *(Dryoscopus cubla)*. The whip-crack-like call 'wee chaak wee chaak' is most distinctive and often helps to locate this secretive forest-dwelling shrike. When seen, the puff-back shrike's pied plumage, whitish wings and red eyes are obvious and diagnostic features. The rump and lower back feathers are white, elongated and fluffy, but are normally concealed by the closed wings. During breeding displays, however, these fluffy white feathers are raised, transforming the back into a 'powder puff'. Thus the bird gives the impression of being much larger than it really is and this may 'warn off' competitors. This display may also have other functions; for example, in signalling to a mate, indicating alarm, or in repelling an intruding neighbour. The small nest is a neatly constructed cup of roots and grasses lined with plant down and fine grasses. It is usually placed in the fork of a small branch in a tree or bush.

Collared Sunbird *(Anthreptes collaris)*. At close range, the collared sunbird, one of the smallest birds of the forest, also reveals itself as one of the most colourful. Males have a metallic, glossy-green throat which is separated from the bright yellow breast by a narrow, shiny blue collar. This sunbird behaves very much like a warbler and spends most of its time creeping and flitting through the undergrowth in search of food. Though it occasionally sips nectar from forest blooms, it prefers to glean insects from leaves and branches. It also sometimes pecks at berries, and the clusters of fruit on the lichen-covered wild plum shown here no doubt attracted the attention of this female collared sunbird. The nest, suspended from a branch of a tree or bush, is a well camouflaged, pear-shaped structure made from cobwebs, grasses and mosses. Three tiny eggs are laid and take 17 days to hatch.

Bar-throated Apalis *(Apalis thoracica)*. This secretive little warbler occurs in pairs or small parties which creep or flit through the foliage and along branches in search of insects. Caterpillars are particularly favoured. Once spotted, the bar-throated apalis is easily identified by its white eyes, pale underparts and neat black band across its breast. The alarm call is a high-pitched 'pwee pwee', while the song is a soft 'pilliip pilliip'. Many locations serve as suitable nesting sites, the most common being amongst tangled creepers. The nest itself is usually well camouflaged with sticky spider's webs adorned with pieces of moss and lichen. Three or four small eggs are laid and take only 15 days to hatch.

Ashy Flycatcher *(Muscicapa caerulescens)*. This small flycatcher moves restlessly through the forest in pairs or small family parties. It is easily recognized by its uniform blue-grey plumage and small, white eye-stripes. The feeding habits, too, are distinctive. Alert and upright, it perches prominently to keep a sharp look-out for insects. When a suitable meal is spied, it darts out in the typical manner of flycatchers, to snatch the insect with an audible snap of the bill. It then returns immediately to its perch to resume scanning the air for a further morsel. The ashy flycatcher also sometimes drops to the ground to pick up food and may even fly quite high in pursuit of an insect. The call is a quiet 'ziit ziit' or 'swipt swipt'. The song is somewhat grating and unmusical. The nest, clearly shown here, is placed either in a crevice in a tree trunk or amongst thick creepers and is made from mosses and grasses. The three buff-coloured eggs are overlaid with grey and brown streaks.

Ashy Flycatcher